Journey to the Manger

Journey to the Manger

Exploring the Birth of Jesus

Paula Gooder

Fortress Press

Minneapolis

JOURNEY TO THE MANGER
Exploring the Birth of Jesus

Fortress Press Edition © 2016

This book is published in cooperation with Canterbury Press. Interior contents have not been changed.

Library of Congress Cataloging-in-Publication Data
Print ISBN: 978-1-5064-1887-2
eBook ISBN: 978-1-5064-1888-9

The paper used in this publication meets the minimum requirements of American National Standard for Information Services—Permanence of Paper for Printed Library Materials, ANSIZ329.48-1984.

Manufactured in the U.S.A.

Contents

Introduction

The New Testament Scholars Who Stole Christmas

Imagine, if you will, a typical nativity scene. In it, no doubt, there will be a stable. Mary and Joseph will be standing or sitting around a manger in which the baby Jesus lies. Perhaps to one side you will have shepherds, of varying numbers, with assorted lambs, and on the other side three wise men, looking more or less like kings, bearing a single gift each. Above the stable a large star might glisten and there might even be the odd angel hovering in the night sky having not yet returned to heaven after their appearance to the shepherds.

Enter, stage left, the baddie. No I don't mean King Herod – I mean the New Testament scholar, here with the sole intent of spoiling your picture. It isn't entirely our fault. Sometimes it feels as though people want us to chip away at the picture. I have lost count of the times I have been invited to offer my opinion and in doing so to ruin this kind of tableau. 'Tell us,' people insist. 'What is wrong with the scene? Who shouldn't be there?'

As you may know, there are, from the perspective of New Testament studies, a number of problems with the traditional scene: Jesus may not have been born in a stable but in a house; the presence of an inn (with accompanying innkeeper) is unlikely; the shepherds probably didn't visit at the same time as the wise men; the angels appeared on the hills around Bethlehem but probably didn't hang around afterwards; there is no evidence that there were three wise men (only that there were three gifts – these could have been brought by two or 25 people); the wise men were probably not kings; the star may or may not have 'hung' over the place where Jesus lay. Then there are problems of dating. Ironically Jesus may not have been born in the year zero, since Herod the Great died in 4 BC and the major census attributed to Quirinius, governor of Syria, was between AD 6 and 7. Put all of these together and you can begin to feel the Christmas tableau crumble before your very eyes. Over the years New Testament scholars have stripped away details of our beloved nativity scenes until we are left with a few forlorn characters on an entirely unfamiliar stage. No wonder people avoid our company around Christmas time!

Let me be clear from the start: I have no desire in this book to be a New Testament scholarly Grinch, intent on stealing your Christmas away slice by slice. I am a fan of the traditional nativity scene. I attend nativity plays with delight year after year. We have three crib sets in our house, which I set up each year, summoning shepherds, wise men, sheep, oxen, camels, angels and stars to the scene with joyful abandon. While I agree with many of the New Testament scholarly points made about an accurate reading of the text, there is a time and a place for these points and that time and place is not the nativity play, nor even necessarily Christmas morning.

Indeed our traditional portrayals of the Christmas story draw on ancient and respectable interpretative traditions, which encourage an imaginative inhabitation of the text. These traditions, found in both Judaism and Christianity, encourage us to imagine further details about the story, to see with our mind's eye not only the characters mentioned in the text but others too. A nativity play that stayed faithful to exactly what we can find in either Luke or Matthew would be very short and a little disappointing.

In my view there is nothing wrong at all with supplying additional details or with conflating the accounts of Matthew and Luke together, so long as we do not forget that this is what we have done. If we remain clear that extra characters, additional details and conflation of stories are necessary to make the story easier to engage with, then there is little wrong with that. The problems arise when our additions to the narrative are taken as seriously as, or more seriously than, the original itself.

The key question is at what point we mention this fact. It is easy to work out which are the wrong occasions in which to mention this, much harder to work out which are the right ones. A book such as this is surely one of those right occasions, so long as you know that it is not designed to tell you what you can or cannot think about Christmas or the birth narratives. Christmas presents to us, mostly in narrative form, some of the most wonderful truths about our faith – truths about a God who loves us, who was prepared to risk everything to live among us in human form, who drew the most unlikely people to him by doing this and who continues today to seek to draw people to him from all walks of life. Christmas is a feast that encourages our imaginative engagement with the mysterious truths it seeks to portray – and no one has the right to criticize the invitation to imaginative engagement.

At the same time, Christmas can also raise for us serious problems about the nature of this engagement. For those who know the biblical stories (and there are not as many as there used to be), one of the greatest barriers to deep theological reflection is overfamiliarity. When we know the stories too well, it is very difficult to read them with fresh eyes. When the narratives become too much a part of our inner world, we come to them encumbered by half-remembered reflections of years gone by, years of interpretation through nativity plays and crib services and centuries of Christian art, so that it becomes almost impossible to read them as they are for what they might have to say to us.

The purpose of this book is not to be prescriptive. It does not seek to tell you what can and cannot be believed. Instead it seeks to be suggestive, to open up new ways of seeing these well-known and well-loved stories and to read the text in detail so that we can encounter afresh some of what it tells us that has become lost beneath layers of overfamiliarity.

On History and Historicity

It is almost impossible these days to study the New Testament without asking questions of history and historicity. Questions abound about when events took place; when stories were captured in oral or written form; when the Gospels reached their final form and so on. These questions have been incredibly helpful in shaping our understanding of the New Testament world and how the texts reached us in the form that they did. However, they only take us so far. They explain the origins of the biblical books we read but they do not always offer much help on what they actually mean. By and large in the pages that follow we will be much more interested in what the text means than in when it was written. We cannot, however, avoid history entirely. The birth narratives raise particular questions for us about history and historicity – when exploring the birth narratives of Jesus we simply cannot help bumping up against them. Specific questions – such as the dates of Herod the Great and the great census of Governor Quirinius – we can explore as they arise in the text, but we need first to spend a moment reflecting on more general issues about historicity.

Here we cannot help but struggle with widely differing but firmly held views. For some people the birth narratives are historically true in every detail; for others they are fictional in whole or in part. In fact the choice often offered to us is whether we deem them fact or fable. So strongly do people hold the opposing views that they hold, that it is often difficult even to begin talking about the issues surrounding this question. This book does not seek to persuade you to take one side or another – indeed I am yet to be persuaded that the choice is an either/or one. It is up to you to decide what you think – or even to decide that you can't decide right now. I will tell you what I think shortly, but before I do, let us explore the issues that raise the question in the first place.

One of the issues often raised by those questioning the historicity of the birth narratives is that the accounts themselves are really quite different. Only two of the four Gospels report Jesus' birth at all, and the two that do give quite different accounts. Luke focuses on Mary's story; Matthew concentrates on Joseph. Luke has the shepherds visit the baby; Matthew the wise men. Matthew tells the story of the threat to Jesus' life after his birth; Luke makes no mention of this at all. Herod the Great plays a key role in

Matthew; in Luke he does not. In Luke Mary appears to live in Nazareth before the birth of Jesus; in Matthew Mary and Joseph seem to settle there only after their return from Egypt.

The contrasts between the accounts are great but it is important not to overstate them. There is remarkable overlap: the name of Jesus' mother is Mary in both accounts and the name of his adoptive father is Joseph; both Matthew and Luke assert the virginal conception of Jesus and that he was born in Bethlehem; both recount that his birth was announced by angels and that visitors were guided to where he was. The differences are certainly pronounced but we should not overlook the key similarities either.

The similarities dictate that the accounts cannot simply be attributed to a burst of creativity by either Matthew or Luke. There is a strong 'base' tradition about the birth of Jesus that holds in common the identity of his parents; that Mary was a virgin when he was conceived; that the Holy Spirit was the agent in his conception; that he grew up in Nazareth but was born in Bethlehem; that his birth was announced by supernatural intervention (angels in Luke and an angel and a star in Matthew); that he was visited by surprising guests after his birth. All in all these overlapping details indicate that there was some level of agreed tradition about the circumstances surrounding Jesus' birth on which both Matthew and Luke drew.

At this point it is worth reminding ourselves that it is much easier to record and retain details about someone after their significance is widely recognized than it is before. If the accounts of Jesus' birth do not match in every detail, this could simply be because his birth became more important in people's minds only once he was an adult. Despite the excitement his and John's births created, it is highly unlikely that their every move was watched from their birth onwards in expectation of the moment they would reveal themselves to the world. It is much more likely that once people worked out who they were as adults, memories of their births were recalled. This does not necessarily mean that the reports are 'unhistorical' but that they are dependent even more than the rest of the Gospel accounts on memory of times past.

The problem with this is that it can sometimes be difficult to recall precise – though important – detail.

Another point often made is the strong connection between the accounts of Jesus' birth and Old Testament references. This is especially true of Matthew but can also be said of Luke. There can be no doubt that there are strong and compelling parallels between Matthew's account and the Old Testament. Particularly striking is the clear resonance between Isaiah 60, verses 3 and 6, and the account of the magi's visit to Jesus. This has caused a good number of scholars to conclude that Matthew has stitched together his account of Jesus' birth from various Old Testament stories – including Numbers 22—24; 2 Samuel 5.2; Micah 5.2; Psalm 72.10, 15, as well as Isaiah 60.3, 6.

It is here that we need to remember something important about the nature of history in the minds of Matthew and Luke. As becomes clear when we turn our attention to genealogies in Chapter 1 below, Matthew and Luke have a very different view of history from that of the modern world. In fact it may not be too much of an exaggeration to observe that their view of history is the opposite of ours. In our context, something copied or borrowed from the past might be considered less true rather than more true; in the ancient world the opposite was the case. If you could prove that the story you told was old or that the roots of your beliefs went far back into history, this would demonstrate that what you said was reliable and trustworthy. This is why, for example, when Josephus told the story of Judaism to the Romans in his *Antiquities of the Jews*, he went out of his way to stress how ancient their story was – the more ancient the more reliable it was.

Oddly this is why we find ourselves with the problems we do in determining the historicity of the birth narratives. The very things Matthew and Luke believed would support the veracity of their narratives undermine them for us. In my view it is not that Matthew was making up his story but that he told the story with the particular intention of demonstrating how it fulfilled many Old Testament texts therefore proving, in his mind, that Jesus was who Matthew said he was. If there had been no passages to support his story, Matthew might well have felt that his argument about who Jesus was was not so strong. The central problem that we face as modern readers is precisely this: what Matthew and Luke needed to do to prove the truth of their narrative to their audience – that this was a story with ancient roots – actually raises questions for us about whether their accounts can be trusted.

There are many people today who struggle to accept the historicity of the birth narratives. There can be no doubt that the narratives raise some very challenging questions about historicity, but we need to be careful not to overexaggerate them. In my view (and it really is only my view; you can decide whether to agree with me or not), we have a tendency to be like the Pharisees in Matthew 23.24 who strain out gnats but swallow camels. The birth narratives are about the mind-blowing, brain-boggling truth that the God who shaped the universe into existence was prepared to be born as a tiny, vulnerable baby. This God trusted his whole well-being to a young girl, who had never had a baby before and wasn't even married. This God chose a ludicrously risky means of redeeming the world he loved so much. Whenever I think about this my brain is so taken up with the wonder and mystery of it that there is minimal space left for the historical questions that seem to trouble others so deeply.

Of course, you may respond that the veracity – or not – of the birth narratives proves or disproves the theological points I've just laid out. This may be true if we were able to come to a final, indisputable position about the issues raised. If we could prove beyond a shadow of a doubt that the facts of Jesus' birth were entirely fictional in all parts it might – but only might – undermine the wondrous theology we explore at Christmas. The problem is that we can't prove them to be true any more than we can prove them to be false. This is why I am driven back time and time again to the theology of what they tell us about Jesus – which is something we can continue talking about – over and against historical discussions that regularly end up in an 'Oh yes it did happen'/'Oh no it didn't' impasse.

The key thing here is to reflect for yourself on how you relate to these questions and how important you consider them to be. You may decide that it is vital for your faith that you believe all of the features of the birth narratives exactly as they are portrayed in every detail. You may decide that it is vital for your faith to believe none of the features of the birth narratives. Or, like me, you may take a roughly middle position, believing the fundamentals to be true but being less concerned about some of the more problematic details. I know many devout Christians who fall into each of these categories. What is important is that you work it out for yourself.

Personally I see no reason at all why the birth narratives couldn't have happened roughly as Luke and Matthew describe. I recognize that there are problems with some details, and we will explore each of these as they come up in the text, but over-all there is, as we have already seen, notable agreement between the two accounts about some of the fundamental details of Jesus' birth. If I find myself with any time for further reflection on the issues surrounding Jesus' birth, I would much rather meditate on John 1.1–18 in all its beauty than try to work out how much of Matthew's account happened exactly as he said it did. If you find this approach unsatisfactory, you may like to turn your attention to some of the books in the Further Reading section at the end of this one, most of which explore the history question in much more detail than I do.

The Snowball of History

In my book *The Meaning is in the Waiting*, I've described my view of the way Old Testament history works, but it feels as though it may be helpful to restate it here as it sheds light on what is going on in the birth narratives and why they appear to be so concerned to link their stories to Old Testament texts.

One of the reasons why modern readers of the Bible often struggle with its narrative is because of a difference between how we see the unfolding of time. Most modern people see history as linear: beginning at one point and moving forward. Some modern views of the world also think that humanity progresses onwards as history unfolds. This is not how the biblical writers saw it. Although there is certainly an element of development and moving

forward, there was also a strong belief in repetition – that events
that had happened in the past would happen again and again. In
particular this seems to be how the biblical writers understood the
history of salvation. God's intervention in history to redeem and
to save his people was seen as repeated action, happening time
and time again through history.

The place where this becomes most apparent is in Psalm
74.12–15:

> Yet God my King is from of old,
> working salvation in the earth.
> [13]You divided the sea by your might;
> you broke the heads of the dragons in the waters.
> [14]You crushed the heads of Leviathan;
> you gave him as food for the creatures of the wilderness.
> [15]You cut openings for springs and torrents;
> you dried up ever-flowing streams.

This passage is intriguing because it is almost impossible to work
out which one event is being referred to. The mention of crushing
the heads of Leviathan appears to suggest that this is a reference
to creation;[1] dividing the sea by might suggests the Exodus; opening springs and torrents suggests the wilderness wanderings. The
fact that they are thoroughly intertwined here implies that in the
mind of the Psalmist they are the same event played out at different times.

In the same way the Gospel writers seem to have a similar idea
when writing the birth narratives. Jesus' birth is a moment in
which all the great acts of God's salvation are brought together –
it is the same event again, but in a very special way. Jesus is the
new Abraham, the new Moses, the new Samson, the new Samuel,
he is the return from exile and the moment when the Davidic line
begins to rule again. He is all those moments made present again

---

1 Leviathan was a legendary sea monster. God's defeat of that monster
as a part of creation is referred to a few times in the Psalms.

in a unique way because this time God himself is present on earth as a human being.

The image I often use to illustrate this is that of a snowball. If you made a snowball and put a stone in it on the top of a hill and then rolled it down the hill, every time the snowball turned the stone would gain a new layer of snow. The stone would remain as it was but it would have layer after layer of snow on top of it. In my view God's salvation is viewed like this in the Bible. It is the same event simply with new layers on top of it every time it happened again.

I feel that to suggest that the birth narratives are no more than a rehash of a smorgasbord of Old Testament texts is to miss the point entirely. Matthew and Luke are proving to us that this is the grand moment of salvation, the moment when God's intervention in the world happens yet again but in an entirely new way. In order to prove this they *need* to use Old Testament texts, stories and references to demonstrate that this is a genuine act of God's salvation re-enacted before our eyes. They saw the events that unfolded as repetitions of what had happened before.

For Matthew and Luke, the Old Testament allusions, resonances and quotations are the very point of their story. This is the old, old story of God loving his people, calling them back to him, dwelling in their midst, but this time in a way like never before. The story only makes sense if we can look backwards and see how it is both profoundly familiar and profoundly unfamiliar at the same time.

What's in the Book and How to Read It

A brief glance at the Contents list will tell you that I have allowed myself latitude on what we can legitimately put under the heading 'birth narratives'. Indeed you could easily argue that Parts 1 and 2 of the book are not really birth narratives at all. Part 1 is about origins – where Jesus came from. Both Matthew and Luke have a genealogy that attempts to paint a picture of Jesus' human origins, origins that take us back to the ancestors of life and faith (Abraham and Adam). John's Gospel does something similar but in a completely different way. John's prologue is, in my view, a theological genealogy that matches to perfection the human genealogies of Matthew and Luke. The genealogies trace Jesus' human ancestry; John's prologue traces his divine origins. While not strictly birth narratives, this material gets us ready for the birth and person of Jesus.

On one level Part 2 is even harder to justify. It is about the announcements of John's birth to Zechariah and Jesus' to Mary and to Joseph. Chronologically they took place between 15 and 9 months before Jesus' birth and therefore are not 'birth narratives' by any stretch of the imagination (though John's birth is recorded at the end of Luke 1). Nevertheless these stories are integrally linked to the birth narratives because they prepare us for the birth and all that it will mean. It is almost impossible to explore Jesus' birth if we exclude the announcements of that birth – some of the key details, like the virginal conception, would be missing – and so I have included them.

The final two parts of the book are more 'traditional' Christmas fare exploring Jesus' birth and the varying welcomes he received.

I have allowed the material – rather than a predetermined figure – to decide the length of the chapters. It proved artificial and unsatisfactory, for example, to make the chapter about John's birth as long and important as the one about Jesus' birth. I wrestled with the question for a while but in the end decided that the texts we were reading were more important than keeping to a nice neat chapter division.

The varying lengths of the chapters may affect how you read them. It may be easier to dip in and out looking for particular sections than to read them all the way through. Some people may be looking for a book to read during Advent; for you I have split the material into four sections, one for each week. Alternatively you could read this in Advent and Christmas, saving the post-Christmas material for later on.

Some may want to use this book in a book group or in Bible study. It is to you I offer the greatest apology since some weeks will involve more arduous reading than others. In the back of the book I have included questions to kick-start discussion. They allow you to focus either on a particular passage – John's prologue; the annunciation to Mary; Luke's birth narrative; the worship of the magi – or on more of the passages in each part. You could if you wanted only read the relevant section of the book for your discussion. The questions are very much only springboards to get a discussion started – your group will need to generate more questions to keep it going for an hour or more. Given the material, though, this shouldn't be a problem!

The main body of the book takes the form of a deep engagement with the biblical text; I have aimed for something that falls between a commentary and a thematic book. The relevant passages are reproduced, and I have taken what seem to me to be the most interesting discussions about the text in New Testament commentaries and gathered them together. Of course, what strikes me as interesting may not be the same as what you consider to be interesting; there are also a number of places where it is impossible to decide authoritatively how to resolve a knotty issue.

Dotted throughout the book, in a different font, are my own reflections evoked by the passages I have been exploring. There is at least one in each chapter but sometimes more, depending on the subject matter of the chapter. At the end of each part of the book I have written a meditative response inspired by my own reading of the text. I am not a poet and they are not poetry; they simply represent a different way of responding to the text.

The birth narratives introduce us for the first time to Jesus Christ, Son of God, Saviour and Lord. They give us an initial answer to that question – 'Who is this?' – that runs all the way through the Gospels. The birth narratives lay out in story, in poetry and in song something of what we believe about this Jesus, Immanuel, God with us. They help us to think imaginatively and creatively about the one we worship, who came to us in the most precarious manner possible – born as a baby into poverty. They are stories worth savouring since they tell us how the world was transformed 2,000 years ago by the God of love and how that same God will, if only we can let him, transform us too.

PART 1

Origins

When we think about the stories of Jesus' birth it is easy to see them as the stories of his origins. Three out of the four Gospels, however, are very clear that this is not the case – or at least not entirely. For each of them, in their different ways, the origins of Jesus stretched back far beyond his birth by Mary. Matthew and Luke tell this story in a somewhat uninspiring, functional way (few of us would choose to read the genealogies for fun!), but John takes the opportunity to engage in a beautiful, mind-expanding piece of theology that introduces us to the deep truths of God and Christ. The extreme contrast in style between Matthew and Luke's genealogies and John's prologue is only exacerbated by placing them next to each other in the same part of this book. At the same time, thematic overlaps come to the fore and so suggest avenues for further reflection.

1

The Genealogies of Matthew and Luke

The genealogies are not, to put it mildly, exciting stuff. Long lists of names that stretch back to Abraham or Adam are hardly at the top of anyone's inspirational spiritual reading. Nevertheless they are important to both Matthew and Luke's stories and we cannot really understand the opening of the Gospels without them.

Genealogies were a common feature of the ancient world. Being able to trace family back to ancient origins gave people a sense of identity and stability. The success of the BBC television programme *Who do you think you are?* and the abiding popularity of tracing family trees remind us that this is not just true of the ancient world. Even today, knowing something about your family and where you came from can contribute to a sense of where you fit in the world.

There were many genealogies in Greek biographies of famous people but it is most likely that those in Matthew and Luke were inspired by the genealogies of the Old Testament. There are a couple dotted through Genesis (5.1–31; 11.10–32), as well as a lengthy one at the start of 1 Chronicles (chapters 1—9).

The similarity between them and those in the Gospels suggests that Matthew and Luke were consciously mimicking them. In their different ways, through the language they used, the allusions to Old Testament writing and events they employed as well as the whole style in which they cast their narratives, both Matthew and Luke suggest that what they are writing is not a new story but a sequel to the Old Testament narratives. The genealogies focus our recognition of this in Matthew before the rest of his Gospel begins, and in Luke between the birth narratives and the start of Jesus' ministry.

Matthew's Genealogy

Matthew 1.1–17 An account of the genealogy of Jesus the Messiah, the son of David, the son of Abraham.

²Abraham was the father of Isaac, and Isaac the father of Jacob, and Jacob the father of Judah and his brothers, ³and Judah the father of Perez and Zerah by Tamar, and Perez the father of Hezron, and Hezron the father of Aram, ⁴and Aram the father of Aminadab, and Aminadab the father of Nahshon, and Nahshon the father of Salmon, ⁵and Salmon the father of Boaz by Rahab, and Boaz the father of Obed by Ruth, and Obed the father of Jesse, ⁶and Jesse the father of King David.

And David was the father of Solomon by the wife of Uriah, ⁷and Solomon the father of Rehoboam, and Rehoboam the father of Abijah, and Abijah the father of Asaph, ⁸and Asaph the father of Jehoshaphat, and Jehoshaphat the father of Joram, and Joram the father of Uzziah, ⁹and Uzziah the father of Jotham, and Jotham the father of Ahaz, and Ahaz the father of Hezekiah, ¹⁰and Hezekiah the father of Manasseh, and Manasseh the father of Amos, and Amos the father of Josiah, ¹¹and Josiah the father of Jechoniah and his brothers, at the time of the deportation to Babylon.

¹²And after the deportation to Babylon: Jechoniah was the father of Salathiel, and Salathiel the father of Zerubbabel, ¹³and Zerubbabel the father of Abiud, and Abiud the father of Eliakim, and Eliakim the father of Azor, ¹⁴and Azor the father of Zadok, and Zadok the father of Achim, and Achim the father of Eliud, ¹⁵and Eliud the father of Eleazar, and Eleazar the father of Matthan, and Matthan the father of Jacob, ¹⁶and Jacob the father of Joseph the husband of Mary, of whom Jesus was born, who is called the Messiah.

¹⁷So all the generations from Abraham to David are fourteen generations; and from David to the deportation to Babylon, fourteen generations; and from the deportation to Babylon to the Messiah, fourteen generations.

In his genealogy Matthew points us back to Abraham. It is not hard to work out why. For Matthew, Abraham – the father of Judaism – began the story of faith and faithfulness to God that his story of Jesus now picks up.

The introduction to the genealogy has an odd formula. It feels clunky and out of place. The Greek says '*biblos geneseōs Iēsou Christou*'. This is almost impossible to put well into English, hence the NRSV's slightly lame 'An account of the genealogy of . . .'. A better though less clear translation would be something like 'Book of the origins of . . .' or even 'Book of the Genesis of . . .'. It is certainly intriguing that Matthew chose to use the Greek title of the first book of the Bible, 'Genesis', to open his genealogy. It feels as though he is drawing our attention here to Genesis, with its story of beginnings. If he is, then he is directing us to think of his story as a new beginning – a new creation.

This connection is especially highlighted when you realize that the creation story beginning at Genesis 2.4 and the genealogy at Genesis 5.1 both open in the Greek translation of the Septuagint with this same phrase, '*biblos geneseōs*'. It is almost as though Matthew is making a verbal connection with Genesis and reminding his readers that this new tale unfolding before them is both an ancient story that reaches back to the dawn of time and also the start of something entirely new.

Three lots of fourteens

The first thing to jump out of Matthew's genealogy – not least because Matthew explicitly draws our attention to it in 1.17 – is that it is made up of three lots of fourteen. You will notice that at the end of each of the lots of fourteen something significant happened: 1.6–7 notes the kingship of David and 1.11 the start of the exile. The implication of this is that at the end of this last batch of fourteen generations the time was ripe for something else to happen – something significant that would be at least as world-changing as the reign of David and the departure into exile in Babylon.

Matthew makes much of the two numbers he uses here – three and fourteen – so it is natural for us to attempt to work out why they were so important. The number three is relatively easy to understand. It runs all the way through the Old Testament: people have three children (Noah in Genesis 6.10 and Job in Job 1.2); people bow down or pray in threes (David in 1 Samuel 20.41 and Daniel in Daniel 6.10); three days are often important (Exodus 15.22), as are three months (Exodus 2.3). In all of these it is traditional to take the number three as a symbol of completeness.

In rabbinic discussion the number three was seen to symbolize a harmony that includes, synthesizes and completes two opposites. Although the discussions date from a later period than Matthew, you can't help wondering whether this is what is happening here. If we take the end of each period of fourteen we have the good of David's reign against the bad of the exile, all brought together in the completeness of the true King in whom all the nations of the earth can find their homecoming. That Jesus comes to complete the third of three sets of fourteen suggests not only completeness but the reconciliation of the golden days of David with the dark days of exile.

The number fourteen causes us more problems because its significance is harder to fathom. Two of the explanations provided are tantalizing, and you will need to decide for yourself whether you are persuaded by either, both or neither of them. The first is that a full cycle of the moon lasts for 28 days: fourteen waning and fourteen waxing. One theory, then, is that the first fourteen generations were a period of waxing reaching its peak in David; followed by a period of waning reaching its nadir at the exile. This would make the final period of fourteen another period of waxing, reaching a new peak with the birth of Christ.

Another explanation is taken from rabbinic exegesis. Something called *gematria* was common among the rabbis. *Gematria* is a complex mix of maths and theology. Each Hebrew letter was assigned a number (one for *aleph*, two for *beth* and so on). The rabbis would add the numbers in words together to make a sum they would then associate with other words that made a similar sum. If you add together the numbers associated with the consonants of David's name (4+6+4 = 14) you get fourteen (in case you are confused, the Hebrew letter *vav*, which is the middle consonant of David's name, is the sixth letter of the Hebrew alphabet). Some have also commented, in the light of Matthew's genealogy, that there may be significance in the fact that there are three consonants in David's name – three and fourteen then being suggested by the same name.

The fanciful nature of these explanations suggests that, in reality, scholars do not really know why fourteen was so important to Matthew, but whatever the explanation, it is clear that he believed the time was ripe for God to act again. His genealogy is designed to persuade us of this too. Poised at the end of three lots of fourteen generations, anyone who knew their history would have been ready and waiting for God to act.

The four women of Matthew's genealogy

The other striking feature of Matthew's genealogy is that, in a list otherwise exclusively male, four women are included: Tamar (1.3); Rahab (1.5); Ruth (1.5) and Bathsheba (1.6). Not only are they women but each of them is notorious in her own way. Tamar resorted to a dubious subterfuge to trick her father-in-law into having sex with her so that her children could be counted as the children of her dead husband; Rahab was a prostitute who was willing to betray her city in order to protect the Israelites; Ruth, a Moabite, lay down 'at the feet' of Boaz (a phrase some take to be a euphemism for his genitals); and Bathsheba committed adultery with David.

As you can imagine, there has been much debate about the significance of the inclusion of these women, and there is little agreement about what they signify. My own view is that these women are included to defend Mary against any accusations of unworthiness. Like her, they could all be accused of moral failing in one way or another, according to the customs of their day, but despite that they remain a vital part of the grand story of God's people. Whatever the cultural attitudes that prevail, these women cannot be written out of God's story any more than Mary could.

If anyone wanted to claim that Jesus could not be who Matthew believed him to be because of suspicions surrounding the morals of Mary, the answer was simply that David was born from a line equally questionable. Not only that, but David's own relationship with Bathsheba raised similar, if not even greater, moral questions.

Matthew's genealogy seems to set out to remind us that God acted and continues to act in history in and through the most questionable of people. Where human beings might be tempted to write them out of the narrative in order to keep the story pristine, God's choice time and time again of the dubious, the outcasts and the marginal insists that they be written back in and remain at the heart of his story of love. We may be able to expunge one or two from this story, but as Matthew reminds us here, there are simply too many valiant, admirable, determined women in the story from Abraham to Jesus to silence. Mary did not stand alone. She stood with her forebears in the faith, a rightful heir of God's blessing alongside Tamar, Rahab, Ruth and Bathsheba.

* * *

Reflection

I love the idea of these four standing as defenders of Mary's reputation. I have a mental image of this slightly rag-bag bunch of women, battered by life and what they had needed to do to survive it, standing shoulder to shoulder, chins lifted high, defiance in their eyes ready to defend the young Mary from accusations of unworthiness and disrepute.

I love even more the idea that into this picture we need to insert God: the God who protected them all and reassures both them and us that we have no need to defend Mary because he chose her specially; that she as well as Tamar, Rahab, Ruth and Bathsheba plays a vital part in his plan for the world; that despite what people might say, it is and remains a good plan. It was a plan that needed Tamar just as much as it needed Judah; Rahab as much as Salmon; Ruth as much as Boaz; Bathsheba as much as David. It is a plan that needs us. Whoever we are, however ramshackle and dubious we might be, the God who needed Judah and Tamar, Rahab and Salmon, Boaz and Ruth, David and Bathsheba and Mary and Joseph needs us to be a part of his plan.

No one needs to defend anyone else – all we need to do is hear and respond to God's call on our lives and to remind ourselves that unworthy as we may feel, we join a long string of people others deemed unacceptable and God declared to be just right.

* * *

Luke's Genealogy

Luke 3.23–38 Jesus was about thirty years old when he began his work. He was the son (as was thought) of Joseph son of Heli, [24]son of Matthat, son of Levi, son of Melchi, son of Jannai, son of Joseph, [25]son of Mattathias, son of Amos, son of Nahum, son of Esli, son of Naggai, [26]son of Maath, son of Mattathias, son of Semein, son of Josech, son of Joda, [27]son of Joanan, son of Rhesa, son of Zerubbabel, son of Shealtiel, son of Neri, [28]son of Melchi, son of Addi, son of Cosam, son of Elmadam, son of Er, [29]son of Joshua, son of Eliezer, son of Jorim, son of Matthat, son of Levi, [30]son of Simeon, son of Judah, son of Joseph, son of Jonam, son of Eliakim, [31]son of Melea, son of Menna, son of Mattatha, son of Nathan, son of David, [32]son of Jesse, son of Obed, son of Boaz, son of Sala, son of Nahshon, [33]son of Amminadab, son of Admin, son of Arni, son of Hezron, son of Perez, son of Judah, [34]son of Jacob, son of Isaac, son of Abraham, son of Terah, son of Nahor, [35]son of Serug, son of Reu, son of Peleg, son of Eber, son of Shelah, [36]son of Cainan, son of Arphaxad, son of Shem, son of Noah, son of Lamech, [37]son of Methuselah, son of Enoch, son of Jared, son of Mahalaleel, son of Cainan, [38]son of Enos, son of Seth, son of Adam, son of God.

Journeying backwards

Luke's genealogy is about as different from Matthew's as one covering the ancestry of the same person could be. Matthew's began with Abraham and worked forward to Jesus; Luke's began with Joseph and worked backwards to Adam. The first difference is easy to explain. For Matthew, with his more Jewish interest, it is natural that he would want to trace Jesus' ancestry back to Abraham, the father of Judaism; Luke on the other hand, with a concern more for a Gentile audience, would want to demonstrate that Jesus' ancestry stretched back to Adam the father of all humankind.

In Luke's case there may also be a significant theological point being made, which is that Jesus, Son of God, was also profoundly human. The ability to trace his ancestry back to the father of all humankind allowed Luke to make a point about Jesus' humanity right at the start of his adult ministry, and to plant the seed in his readers' minds that he was about to tell the story of the second Adam.

'But Joseph wasn't his biological father!'

– I hear you cry. One of the big problems of both genealogies is that Jesus' ancestry is traced through Joseph who, the birth narratives go to great lengths to prove, was not Jesus' biological father. Surely the whole point of the genealogies is undermined by this simple fact?

Actually for us it would be, but for Matthew and Luke this was clearly not a problem. Here we find ourselves meeting one of those great cultural clashes that from time to time disrupt our ability to understand what is going on in a biblical passage. The key here is adoption in the ancient world. Adoption was widespread within both Roman and Jewish society.

The difference between Roman and Jewish adoption was that in Roman society it was normally of adult men, whereas in Jewish society adoption of babies was more common. The Roman attitude seems to be linked to infant mortality rates and the desire to leave inheritances in safe hands. Adopting a male adult meant that they had already passed through the perilous childhood years and were more likely to survive.

Where Roman and Jewish attitudes to adoption overlap, however, is in the importance ascribed to the act of adoption. For both societies adoption was absolute, and the adoptee was to be treated as though they were the biological child of the new parents. Legally and formally, then, they were treated as a part of that new family. In the case of Jesus, Joseph was his legal, formally recognized father, part of which meant that Jesus shared with him his ancestry.

Another key difference between Matthew and Luke's genealogies is that Luke's is in a completely different place within his narrative than Matthew's is within his. The placing of Matthew's genealogy makes sense, even if it doesn't produce the most exciting opening for a Gospel. Luke's is a little more confusing. It is located not only after the announcements of the birth of Jesus and the birth itself, but after John the Baptist has begun proclaiming his message in the wilderness.

Some scholars argue that a first edition of Luke began with 3.1 and John the Baptist's ministry. Therefore the genealogy placed just before the appearance of Jesus tells us who he was before Luke went back and added more about the birth narratives. Another possibility is that Luke put it here to aid further reflection after the birth narratives. Luke's account of John's birth makes it very clear that John was of a priestly line; the genealogy points us to Jesus' descent from a kingly line. It may be that its location here prepares us to meet Jesus, the King, alongside his cousin, descended from priests, both in the desert, both proclaiming kingship and worship in terms never previously seen.

The different names in the lists

So far so good. It is not hard to appreciate the theological purpose and significance of the genealogies, but they do raise some troubling questions about accuracy. The problem occurs when we look more carefully at the lists themselves: the names on the two genealogies are almost entirely different between the time of David and Jesus. Even Joseph's father is given a different name. This raises the rather important question about the reliability of the genealogies. There has been a vast amount of discussion about this among scholars and little agreement. Two possible theories to explain the differences are that one represents Mary's line and the other Joseph's (Annius of Viterbo argued that Matthew contained Joseph's line and Luke, Mary's), and that the confusion had arisen because of the citation of male names throughout. Another possibility, which may be a little more attractive, is that Matthew represents the descent of the kings in the Davidic line and Luke the actual descendants of David in the branch of Joseph's family from which he came. In other words although from the Davidic line, Joseph was not descended from the kings in that line but from other sons. One genealogy traced the 'official Davidic line'; the other Joseph's actual line.

'As was supposed'

A pleasing little detail is the addition of the small phrase *hōs enomizeto*, which means literally 'as was supposed' or 'as was believed'. In other words Luke is hinting to us that he isn't entirely sure himself and that this is popular tradition. It may help us feel a little better about the discrepancies.

The problem, of course, was that there were no databases of information in the first century. While there is some evidence that priestly families kept a tally of their ancestry in order to demonstrate their purity, there were no central, common lists. As a result traditions about how ancestry could be traced back were dependent on oral, family history. The most likely explanation of the difference is that Matthew and Luke had different sources to work from and so, inevitably, ended up with different lists.

* * *

Reflection

People will respond differently to the challenges thrown up by the genealogies: some will be deeply troubled about the discrepancies and will worry that this reveals a fundamental lack of reliability in the Gospel accounts; others will be much less concerned. There is, in all honesty, no easy solution to the issue – if there had been, someone would have provided it by now. For the past 2,000 years, readers of Matthew and Luke's genealogies have attempted, struggled and then failed to reconcile them. There are a few theories that make the differences more understandable – two of them are outlined above – but no theory removes the problem entirely.

I must admit that I am not someone who is naturally troubled by issues like this. Ancient history is very different from modern history, not least because Matthew and Luke's genealogies emerge out of a world that has few records of any kind. In a world without accurate record-keeping it would have been very hard indeed to compile a genealogy with absolute certainty of its accuracy.

In my view the accuracy of the lists is of much less significance than the point the genealogies were making. This, in both cases, is that Jesus was a part of the long, circuitous story of the history of salvation that began with Adam and found a focus in Abraham, in David and in the exile. The genealogies locate him in this long chain of history but also prepare us for the fact that something momentous is about to happen that will change the world for ever.

It may even be that the messiness of the genealogies points us to truth. From the very dawn of time, God in his infinite wisdom has chosen human beings to bear his message of love in the world. These human beings, from Adam and Abraham onwards, slipped up, made mistakes – deliberate or otherwise – and generally failed to live up to the task God gave them. At the end of a long line of calamity came Jesus, God's own Son, adopted by Joseph into that disastrous, yet beloved, human line. Matthew and Luke's inability even to agree on precisely which line it was may, in fact, prove the point of the riskiness of God's venture.

The trustworthiness of the accounts lies not in whether the Gospel writers got one or two or even 25 names wrong in their lists, it lies in the acknowledgement that Jesus, fully God yet also fully human, came to meet us in the mess, to love us, to save us and to give us a new family tree that can be traced back without a shadow of a doubt to him, the source of all life.

2

The Genealogy of John

You may never have thought of the prologue of John as a genealogy before – and of course it is far more than just that – but read alongside Matthew and Luke's genealogies we find that it has something in common with them. Both Matthew and Luke were attempting to point to the long shadow that lay behind the life and ministry of Jesus, the history of salvation that led up to the moment of his birth. In both cases this long story was shaped by human beings in a chain of history that stretched back many years. John also chose to begin with a long chain of history that stretched backwards. His story, however, was not the human story but the divine story that stretched back beyond even the dawn of time itself. Where Matthew and Luke painted the human ancestry of Jesus, John painted his divine ancestry. The prologue, therefore, fits well in this chapter alongside the genealogies, in as much as it fits with any other Gospel text.

Any sensible commentator quakes before attempting to explore John 1. So much has been written in the past about it that it would almost be impossible to say anything new at all. So profound is its theology that any attempt to explain it must run the risk of diluting what it has to say. So beautiful is its poetry that any words we might use will run the risk of trampling its own words underfoot. Despite this it is important to stop for a while and savour again its beauty and profundity.

Many New Testament scholars are of the opinion that John 1.1–18 is poetic. It might even be a poem or a hymn. Despite that, most English translations lay out the text in prose rather than poetry form. Seeing the prologue laid out like a poem can be an immediate way of seeing it in a different light.

The Prologue

John 1.1–18

In the beginning was the Word,
and the Word was with God,
and the Word was God.
²He was in the beginning with God.

³All things came into being through him,
and without him not one thing came into being.
What has come into being ⁴in him was life,
and the life was the light of all people.
⁵The light shines in the darkness,
and the darkness did not overcome it.

⁶There was a man sent from God,
whose name was John.
⁷He came as a witness to testify to the light,
so that all might believe through him.
⁸He himself was not the light,
but he came to testify to the light.
⁹The true light, which enlightens everyone,
was coming into the world.

¹⁰He was in the world,
and the world came into being through him;
yet the world did not know him.
¹¹He came to what was his own,
and his own people did not accept him.

[12]But to all who received him,
who believed in his name,
he gave power to become children of God,
[13]who were born, not of blood
or of the will of the flesh or of the will of man,
but of God.

[14]And the Word became flesh
and lived among us,
and we have seen his glory,
the glory as of a father's only son,
full of grace and truth.
[15](John testified to him and cried out,
'This was he of whom I said,
"He who comes after me
ranks ahead of me
because he was before me."')
[16]From his fullness we have all received, grace upon grace.
[17]The law indeed was given through Moses;
grace and truth came through Jesus Christ.
[18]No one has ever seen God. It is God the only Son,
who is close to the Father's heart,
who has made him known.

John 1.1–18 and the purpose of the prologue

Laying John 1.1–18 out like this emphasizes the definite poetic rhythm and style of the passage. There are a few verses, however, that do not appear to fit in with the rest. Verses such as 6–9, 13 and 15 are much less poetic and have led some scholars to argue that they are prose insertions. Those who take this view argue that the prologue is made up of an original poem that has been spliced with extra material, particularly about John the Baptist.

They argue that parts of John 1.1–18 were some kind of hymn used in the community of the author, a hymn influenced by the wisdom tradition and in particular Proverbs 8.22–31.

Whether it was originally a hymn of praise to Jesus Christ the eternal Word – into which the material about John the Baptist was inserted at a later date – or written as it now stands, as a prologue to the Gospel, John 1.1–18 functions a little as an overture does in a musical or opera. An overture attunes our ears to what we are about to hear and introduces some of the main melodies that return later in the piece. The prologue does just this. Some of its themes are obvious and easy to spot, such as witnessing or light and darkness; some are more subtle and require greater depth of thought and reflection to identify them here and in the rest of the Gospel.

A theme that requires particular reflection is that of Jesus' divinity. Over the Christian centuries John's Gospel has been criticized fairly regularly for placing much more emphasis on Jesus' divinity than on his humanity. I have never been completely convinced by this criticism.

The problem is not that Jesus is only presented as divine but that the portrayal of his divinity is often separated from that of his humanity. The Gospel itself does not appear to balance them well. At some points in the Gospel, Jesus certainly seems overwhelmingly divine – for example at his arrest in Gethsemane when his words 'I am he' cause the soldiers to fall to the ground (18.5) – but at others he is movingly human and feels exhaustion and thirst (4.6). However, these points rarely if ever meet. They are, however, beautifully balanced in the prologue. In fact they could not really be better balanced than they are here, where Jesus the divine Word became flesh and dwelt among us.

This suggests to me that John's prologue really is a 'prologue' – a fore(pro)word(logue). As a foreword it gives us the clues and tips that will help us read the rest of the Gospel properly, a lens through which to peruse it. It is almost as though we need to have the prologue next to us so that we can make sure we read the Gospel with enough balance, not tipping too much in one direction or the other. If this is true then we can appreciate the prologue as fitting fully, wholly and properly where it is currently placed, providing a beautiful balance of poetry and prose; divinity and humanity in a work of profound theological breadth and depth that helps us read the rest of the Gospel with eyes wide open.

Genesis again

You may remember that Matthew's genealogy makes an apparent allusion to Genesis with its opening phrase: 'Book of the Genesis of Jesus Christ'. He is not alone in drawing this connection with Genesis. John 1.1 also famously makes an allusion to Genesis 1.1 with its opening phrase: 'In the beginning was the Word'. It is also possible that Mark 1.1 alludes to it with its opening: 'The beginning of the good news of Jesus Christ'.

The Greek word *archē* and the Hebrew *bereshit*

The phrase translated as 'in the beginning' here is the phrase *en archē*. This is used by the Greek translators of the Old Testament – in the Septuagint (normally abbreviated LXX) – to translate the first word of the Hebrew in Genesis 1.1, *bereshit*.

The Hebrew word *bereshit* is made up of a preposition meaning 'in', 'on' or 'at' (*be*) and a noun, *reshit*. The Greek *archē* is a remarkably close translation of *reshit*. Both have the resonance of primacy: when used of time they mean 'beginning'; when used in counting they mean 'first'; when used of people they mean 'the head', as in leader.

What is odd about the Hebrew in Genesis 1.1 is that the grammar doesn't work. There are two problems: one is that there is no definite article, 'the' (that is, it says 'in beginning' not 'in the beginning'); the other is that the wrong construction follows. Literally *bereshit* means 'at start of'. In Hebrew the next word should be a noun, and if it had a definite article at the start then the whole phrase would have one. Indeed one might expect the next word to be 'creation' – then the opening phrase would read 'At the beginning of creation . . .' or something like that. The

---

problem is that the next word is a verb: literally 'created God . . .'. So the whole phrase is clunky.

This has led some scholars to wonder whether the opening word *bereshit* is actually the heading of the whole book, not just a temporal description – in other words whether it signals that Genesis as a whole is a story of beginnings. Genesis begins with the grand heading, 'At the start of . . .', and then gives a series of stories that unpack this beginning: creation, the fall, Cain and Abel and so on.

You might think all that detail about a missing 'the' is of little relevance in Genesis 1.1. It may be, but what is striking is that it is also missing in the Gospels. One of the noticeable features of all the allusions to Genesis is the remarkable lack of 'the'. It is missing from the phrase at the start of Matthew; missing again at the beginning of Mark and still absent in John 1.1. Although Matthew 1.1 is not a direct allusion to Genesis 1.1, both Mark 1.1 and John 1.1, as noted above, may well be. Genesis 1.1 might provide a solution to this mysterious case of the missing 'the'. It may be deliberate in the minds of the Gospel writers as a way of ensuring that we recognize that Genesis 1.1 lies behind these verses.

Colossians 1.15–20 and *bereshit*

John 1.1–18 is without doubt the most famous scriptural reflection on Genesis 1.1 but it is not the only one. We have observed already how it is possible that Mark 1.1 may also contain an allusion to Genesis. There is another passage, however, that seems to be deeply steeped in reflections on the Hebrew word *bereshit*. Colossians 1.15–20, like John 1.1–18, is a remarkable piece of poetic theology reflecting on the pre-existent Christ and his role in creation and redemption.

One of the striking features of this passage is that Christ is twice described as 'firstborn' (1.15 and 18), as 'before all things' (1.17) and as 'beginning' (1.18). Each of these words is a legitimate translation of the Hebrew reshit.

Another feature of the passage is that three prepositions are repeated twice: 'in him', 'through him' and 'for him' (1.16 and 1.19–20; the second 'for him' is hidden in the NRSV translation but is present in verse 20 in Greek). All of these are legitimate translations of the Hebrew preposition be at the start of bereshit. Some scholars suggest that Colossians 1.15–20 is a sophisticated scriptural reflection on the first word of Genesis 1.1 in the light of Christ the co-creator and co-redeemer of the world.

If this is true then John 1.1–18 is not alone as a deep spiritual reflection on Scripture – and in particular on Genesis 1 – and may provide us with a pattern on how to reflect deeply on Scripture, savouring it deeply and prayerfully for what it might say to us.

* * *

Reflection

We are accustomed to looking at people's actions as our inspiration for prayer or for the reading of the Bible. So we note that Jesus went off by himself to pray, for example, but I wonder whether we are good enough at observing how the New Testament writers read, savoured and prayed their way through the Old Testament. John 1.1–18 and Colossians 1.1–15 are only two of a great number of New Testament texts that use Old Testament stories, phrases or words as the jumping off point for their prayerful reflection on Christ and the life of faith.

One of the great challenges to us is to ask how we might mimic this prayerful, detailed exploration of Scripture. The practice of Lectio Divina, in which we hear a passage read, meditate upon it, pray with it and contemplate it, goes a little way towards this practice, but what is done in John 1.1–18 and Colossians 1.15–20 goes far beyond this. Here we see a thoughtful, prayerful reflection upon a single – though important – word. This kind of practice takes the practice of *Lectio Divina* to a whole new level.

* * *

Of course a missing 'the' is not the only thing in John 1 that ties it to Genesis 1. John's use of the theme of creation is not found just in 1.1 but continues throughout verses 1–4. One of the key themes here is the life-giving power of The Word. This is one of those themes that is picked up strongly throughout the rest of the Gospel.

It is well known that in John's Gospel the miracles are called 'signs'. They are called signs because they point us to who Jesus really was. As a result they illustrate the many forms of life that spring into being in Jesus' presence. In his presence water becomes wine (2.1–11) and the hungry are fed (6.5–14); the sick are healed (4.46–54) and the lame walk (5.1–18); the blind see (9.1–7) and the dead are raised (11.1–45).

The only one of John's signs that does not appear quite to fit with the rest is Jesus' walking on the water (6.16–24), until you realize that this sign reveals Jesus' power over the waters of chaos. One of the ways creation is described in the Old Testament is as God's combat with the waters of chaos. It is hinted at in Genesis 1.2: 'the earth was a formless void' – literally the words there in Hebrew, *tohu vabohu*, convey both emptiness and confusion – but is stated much more clearly in the Psalms. Psalm 74.12–13, for example, talks about God 'working salvation in the earth', dividing the sea by his might and breaking 'the heads of the dragons in the waters'. The dragons – sometimes called Leviathan – are regarded as the powers of chaos God fought and calmed. When we know this then Jesus' walking on the water in John 6.16–24 fits much better with the rest.

The pre-existent Jesus, who was with God as the world was shaped into being, has creativity at the very core of who he is.

The signs reveal to us who he was, who he is and who he will continue to be. Where Jesus is, life springs forth; the earth gives the best of what it can produce; people are brought back into life, love and community; the powers of chaos cannot hold sway. Just like the genealogies of Matthew and Luke, John's prologue is not just telling us useful pieces of historical information, it is revealing more about who Jesus really is by tracing where he has come from.

Light and darkness

John's theme of creation continues past verses 1–4 into verse 5 with the theme of light and darkness. The separation of light from darkness was, of course, God's first act of creation in Genesis 1 and draws our attention back to the creative act. However, John takes us one step further. Here the light and darkness are not separate. Here the light shines *in* the darkness, battling it as a candle flame in a darkened room. This is creation revisited and reinvigorated through Christ, the light of the world.

One of the key discussions of John 1.5 has been over the translation of the verb *katalambanō*, which the KJV translated as 'comprehend' and the NRSV as 'overcome'. For example:

- And the light shineth in darkness; and the darkness comprehended it not. (KJV)
- The light shines in the darkness, and the darkness did not overcome it. (NRSV)

The problem is that the word can mean both of these. Most modern translations opt for overcome as this is what it seems to mean in the only other place it is used in John ('Walk while you have the light, so that the darkness may not overtake you' 12.35). This, however, does not close the case. It is worth reminding ourselves that this verb can mean both 'comprehend' and 'overcome'/'overtake' because they are closely connected – you comprehend something by overtaking it with your mind. Just before this verse John has been talking about 'The Word'. You may overcome light but you comprehend words. The deep, complex theology this prologue is exploring seems to me to suggest that we accept both meanings here.

The darkness could not overcome/overtake light because darkness is powerless when light shines, but at the same time the moral darkness that had its death-like grip on the world could not begin to comprehend the majesty of the light that had come to dwell in its midst. This is a theme picked up again in verses 9–10, where the prologue states that the world did not know the true light that was coming. This seems most definitely not an either/or but a both/and scenario.

Witnessing to the light

Another strand that runs all the way through not just the prologue but the whole of John's Gospel is the theme of someone sent from God to bear witness to the light.

One of the intriguing things that happens when you put passages together that we don't often think about alongside each other is that some themes become shown in a new light. Here, for me, it is the theme of witnessing. All over the birth narratives in Matthew and Luke there are witnesses who arrive on the scene, sent by God, to reveal to the characters to whom they speak the meaning of key events. In the other Gospels these take the form of angels.

In John's Gospel there are only a few 'angels': some 'ascending and descending upon the Son of Man' in 1.51 and two at the empty tomb in 20.12. There are only a few angels but lots of witnesses and witnessing. In contrast, in Matthew and Luke there are many more angels (especially in Luke) but fewer references to witnessing (in John the noun *marturia*, 'witness', is used 14 times whereas it occurs only four times in the other three Gospels combined, and the verb *marturein*, 'to witness', is used 33 times but only twice in the other Gospels).

The motif may differ but the central point remains the same. The message of the incarnation is so wonderful and hard to comprehend that the human race needed help in discerning it and working out what it meant. In all the Gospels, God provided for this to happen in one form or another, whether by divine or human messenger. It is worth adding that John is clear in 1.6–9 that in reality John the Baptist was a divine messenger because he was sent directly by God to bear witness.

The intimacy of Father and Son

So far we have explored the great themes of creation, of light and darkness, of witnessing, and in the next section we will look at the importance of Jesus' being The Word. Before we get there, there is one more theme we must not overlook. This is the theme of God as Father, Jesus as Son (1.18) and us as children (1.12). In the prologue to John it is clearly an important theme but it is oddly truncated. The first and last we hear of Jesus' divine sonship is in 1.18, and it sits slightly oddly with Jesus The Word, which is the far more commonly cited theme throughout the prologue. Not only that but John introduces the notion of our being children of God six whole verses before Jesus is revealed as son. Elsewhere in the New Testament our status as children of God is heavily dependent on our relationship with Jesus who is Son.

All of this raises the strong suspicion that the author of the prologue assumes that his readers know this tradition of Jesus' being the Son of God and our being the children of God already, and so introduces it briefly and without much fanfare.

It is striking to notice that the word used for our becoming children of God in 1.12 is 'authority' (*exousia*): 'But to all who received him, who believed in his name, he gave power (*exousia*) to become children of God.' This is not the word most of us would use in association with children – 'privilege' maybe, or 'love', but not 'authority' or 'right'. Its use here points us to the way John is using it. The key feature of a child in an ancient household is that the child had a legal standing and hence was able to inherit. Authority is indeed what is needed in this instance. Belief therefore confers on us all familial authority to inherit from God.

On seeing God

John 1.18 has had a strong influence on the popular understanding of the Old Testament tradition about whether it is possible to see God and live. The clear statement 'No one has ever seen God' seems to push us towards the view, backed up by passages like Exodus 33.20 ("But", he said, "you cannot see my face; for no one shall see me and live."), that it is not possible to see the face of God and live.

The problem is that the Old Testament contains a dual tradition: one in which people can see God and the other in which they cannot. The great vision passages like Isaiah 6.1–10, Ezekiel 1.1–28 and even narratives such as Exodus 34.29–35 all suggest that it *is* possible to see God and live. What these passages are all vague on is what of God is seen – either the detail isn't mentioned at all or a vague description is offered (for example, in Ezekiel 1.28 on top of the chariot is 'the appearance of the likeness of the glory of the Lord').

This does not in any way undermine the key point of 1.18, which is that Jesus is the only one who is so close to God that he is in the bosom of the Father. No matter what your reading of the Old Testament tradition is, no one else has ever been described as that close to God.

The language used to describe Jesus' relationship to God as Father is worth a few moments' exploration. The first point to notice is a change in the commonly accepted text of what is written here. The KJV translates this verse as 'No man hath seen God at any time, the only begotten Son . . .'; whereas the NRSV renders this as 'No one has ever seen God. It is God, the only Son . . .'. This reflects modern textual criticism on the verse, which recognizes that the more reliable version – as well as the harder reading – says that Jesus is 'God, the only Son'. This overt divine claim for Jesus fits very easily with the opening of the prologue and explains why it is that Jesus sees God as no one else has seen him.

The other tricky feature of this verse is how to translate the phrase the NRSV has as 'who is close to the Father's heart'. Literally the Greek says 'the one being in/into the bosom/breast/chest/ lap of the Father'. There are a few things to clear up before we start. Unlike the English word 'bosom', *kolpos* is not a particularly gendered term: the same word is used of Abraham's bosom in Luke 16.23. It is a very intimate term and implies intimacy, affection and privilege (it is also used of the disciple who leant on Jesus' bosom in John 13.23).

The other issue is how the preposition *eis* is translated here. Some argue that it just means the same as 'en' or 'in' in English; others that *eis* has particular meaning here of 'into' or 'motion towards'. You can see the effect of the discussion in the different translations offered of this phrase.

'which/who is in the bosom of the Father' (KJV, RSV)
'who is at the Father's side' (NAB and the NIV [1978][1])
'who is nearest to the Father's heart' (NEB, JB)
'who is close to the Father's heart' (NJB, NRSV)

The 2011 NIV has opted for intimacy but dropped the physical imagery: 'who is himself God and is in closest relationship with the Father'.

Most modern scholars would now avoid the first option 'in the bosom of the Father' because it does not have enough motion towards. The question is whether the other options suggest anything either intimate enough or making enough of the affective physical imagery. In my view we are still awaiting a translation that communicates both the intimacy and the movement towards that the Greek suggests.

---

1 The NIV had a radical revision in 2011. '1978' refers to the pre-2011 NIV. It is often interesting to see what changes have been made to the text between the earlier edition and the more modern one.

The Word

There is lots more we could explore in this profoundly rich passage but I would like to end with a reflection on the use of The Word (*ho logos*) to describe Jesus in this passage. As with so much else in John 1, such a lot has been written about Jesus as The Word that it is difficult to know where to begin.

One of the challenges of biblical interpretation is the attempt to work out what might have been in the mind of the writer when he or she wrote. It is an impossible task. It is difficult to know what is in the mind of modern writers when they write, let alone ancient writers. In the case of John's use of *logos*, the big discussion is how much – or whether at all – he was aware of and employing the Greek philosophical usage of *logos*. If he was aware of it then he would have been drawing on Platonic or Stoic ideas, which saw the *logos* as a form or idea or as a rational principle that guided and directed all things.

The Jewish writer Philo was certainly aware of the Greek philosophy behind the word. Philo – a remarkable writer who was born around 25 BC and died around AD 45–50 – lived and worked in Alexandria in Egypt. A deeply devout Jew, he attempted to make sense of the Jewish faith in the light of Greek philosophy. Philo explored the idea of the *logos* as 'thought achieving expression' in both God and humanity. Although he did not believe that the gap between creator and the created was ever bridgeable, the *logos*, that fundamental principle of reason, was what allowed human beings to encounter God.

It is when we recognize in Greek thinking – including that of Philo – the close relationship between *logos* and reason that it becomes clear that this Greek understanding was not John's primary usage of the word. Reason is far from the centre of what John is talking about here. It seems much more likely that what we have in John 1 is, yet again, deep reflections on Genesis 1, probably with the help of the wisdom tradition. In Genesis, creation takes place when God speaks: God says and it is so. God's speech, then, his self-expression, is life-bringing, creative essence. This idea is picked up and explored extensively by the other writers of the Old Testament, for example 'By the word of the Lord the heavens were made' (Psalm 33.6) or 'so shall my word be that goes out from my mouth; it shall not return to me empty, but it shall accomplish that which I purpose, and succeed in the thing for which I sent it' (Isaiah 55.11).

Since God's wisdom was famously personified in Proverbs 8.22–31, it is only a small step from there to the personification of God's word in John 1. It may only be a small step but it is a crucially important one. It is inspiring to think of God's wisdom accompanying the act of creation, rejoicing in its completion and delighting in the human race, but wisdom is largely an internal attribute. Words, by their very nature, are external. They are about self-expression and relationship. The very essence of God is creative, life-bringing self-expression that finds its fulfilment in relationship. Even before God had created the world, The Word existed, ready to craft relationship into being.

One of the Jewish backgrounds sometimes suggested for the *logos* is the Aramaic word *Memra*, which in rabbinic writing is often used to refer to the name of God or to God revealed in the phrase 'I am who I am'. In other words God does not exist in a transcendent, distant way but exists to be at the side of those he has created, always ready to offer love and mercy. John F. McHugh puts it rather beautifully in his ICC commentary on John 1—4: 'The Logos, the Memra, is "He who is there". The sense of John 1.1a is therefore "In the beginning, before the material world was created, there existed the Word of God, the Compassionate, the All-Merciful".'[2]

Whether or not the author of the prologue had the rabbinic use of the word *Memra* in mind when writing, there is no doubt that this theology rather beautifully communicates the essence of what the prologue is saying. Before creation even took place, the God whose very being is love, compassion and relationship was the God who is always there.

---

2 John F. McHugh, *John 1–4*, London: T. & T. Clark, 2008, p. 9.

Eventually even this closeness was insufficient for God, so The Word became flesh and dwelt among us. Just as the word of the Lord came to countless people in the Old Testament, The Word came to our world, became flesh and dwelt among us. This most important phrase in John 1.14 encapsulates the mystery the prologue is circling around here.

At first glance words can seem ephemeral, temporary, here one minute gone the next; in contrast, flesh seems real, permanent and tangible. But John has already unpicked this superficial contrast and continues to unpick it throughout the rest of the Gospel. Verses 1–4 have established the fact that The Word, unlike words, is far from ephemeral and temporary. In fact there is nothing in our world that is more permanent than The Word. The Word has been in existence with God since before our world came into existence. The Word is enduring, everlasting and eternal.

In contrast, flesh is weak and vulnerable. It is fragile and mortal. The contrast is reminiscent of Isaiah 40.6–8, which talks about human constancy as being like the flower of a field, here one minute and gone the next; in contrast to the word of the Lord, which endures for ever. In John 1.14 that which is most enduring chose to become that which is most vulnerable. In this simple phrase 'The Word became flesh', John's prologue sums up all that is encapsulated in Matthew and Luke's birth narratives of the risk of God's choosing to become a baby.

Pitching his tent

It is often pointed out that the word translated as 'lived' in John 1.15: 'The Word became flesh and lived among us' is the Greek word *skēnoō*, which in turn comes from the noun *skēnē* or tent. Thus the verb could be translated as 'he pitched his tent among us'. New Testament scholars often get twitchy about what is known in the trade as etymological fallacies, in other words the assumption that where a word comes from is what it means. This is clearly not the case. Take the word 'understand' in English – it comes from two words 'stand' and 'under'. While you can get from them to the modern usage of 'understand' it is by no means easy. We run the risk of loading words with meanings that they didn't have unless we are careful.

That is the bad news. The good news in this instance is that although that is not really what the word means here, when God did dwell among his people he did do it in the tabernacle, and then the temple. God's dwelling with his people often does take the form of pitching his tent right in the middle of where we are. In this instance the imagery works even though the etymology doesn't.

* * *

Reflection

Words are powerful. They can shape us, affect the way we view not only ourselves but the whole world. The right words at the right time can change the way we look at things, can broaden our horizons and open a door into a new way of being. I am often intrigued by the way words can help you see something in an entirely new way. Something read in a book, heard on the radio, listened to in conversation can break in and break you open. Words can transform you and demand that you are never the same again. They can fire your imagination and help you see beyond fixed certainties.

Conversely the wrong words at the wrong time can be powerfully destructive. That old children's rhyme 'Sticks and stones can break my bones but words can never hurt me' has a nice sentiment but isn't true. The wrong words at the wrong time stick like a burr to the soul, waiting for a low moment to undermine you once more. Words really can hurt, debilitate and wound – and the hurt they cause can last far longer than a mere broken bone.

It is absolutely fitting, therefore, for Jesus to be described as The Word. Jesus is the ultimate right Word coming into the world at the right time, and transforming the whole of the created order. The Word's power to shape, create, transform and heal stands at the heart of what we believe about Christmas. Ever since he came, Christians have been fumbling for words that can in any way capture the revolution that The Word brought to our world. Ever since then we have tried – and mostly failed – to find words that do justice to who he was, who he is and who he continues to be.

John's prologue reminds us that our failure to find the right words is all right. While our words can draw people in – or indeed drive them away – it is not ultimately our words that speak to the heart. We are called not to be 'The Word' but, like John the Baptist, to bear witness, to point beyond ourselves to the one who has always been God's self-expression, bringing new life and new birth to the world.

The task of transformation is not ours. Our task is simply to bear witness, to find the very best words that we can: words that will attract and not repel; words that will illuminate and not confuse; words that open up and not close down. But once we have found – or borrowed – those words, it is our task to fall silent so that the Eternal Word might speak his words of love, joy and hope. After all it is The Word – not our words – that transforms the world.

Meditation

Before the beginning – The Word was
    Before ears or mouths, language or understanding – God was
        ready to speak
    Before people were created – God looked outwards in love
Before the beginning – There The Word was

At the beginning – The Word was
    When life first started to stir – The Word nudged it further
        into life
    When creation emerged into being – The Word fanned the life-
        giving flames
At the beginning – There The Word was

After the beginning – The Word was
    As life gave birth to more life – The Word spoke love and life
    As life turned away from those words – Still The Word spoke
After the beginning – There The Word was

As beginning turned into the middle – The Word was
From Adam to Abraham, from Abraham to David,
from David to Jehoiakim, from Jehoiakim to Joseph
When the right time came – There The Word was, The Word
    made flesh
Before the beginning, at the beginning, after the beginning –
    there The Word was
And There The Word will always continue to be

PART 2

Announcements

It is fairly safe to say that, in Luke's Gospel, Jesus' forthcoming birth does not go underannounced. In terms of preparation, Luke goes out of his way to get us well and truly ready for the birth of Jesus. He begins with the announcement of the birth of Jesus' forerunner, John the Baptist, then the announcement to Mary of Jesus' birth, the visit of Mary to Elizabeth where Mary sings the great Magnificat, the birth of John the Baptist and finally Zechariah's song of praise. By the time we reach the actual birth narratives in Luke 2 we, the readers of Luke's Gospel, have been introduced to many of the key themes that will help us understand who this baby was and what he had come to do.

Matthew, in contrast, is much more restrained in his preparation narratives: they contain the simple account of an angel who appeared to Joseph to tell him not to put Mary aside and to reveal Jesus' name and calling.

3

The Prophecy of John's Birth

The first two chapters of Luke's Gospel, containing the annunciation as well as the accounts of John's and Jesus' births, are markedly different in style from the rest of the Gospel. The Greek changes noticeably in verse 5. The preface, verses 1–4, has a carefully polished, beautiful Hellenistic style – so beautiful, indeed, that they are sometimes said to be four of the most elegant verses in the whole of the New Testament. In verse 5 this style changes suddenly. It moves away from elegant Greek prose to something much more reminiscent of a Hebrew style of writing (though still written in Greek). This style continues for much of chapters 1—2 and only reverts to a more Greek style again in chapter 3, even though it never recaptures the elegance of the first four verses.

This change in style has led people to wonder where Luke got these stories from. Some argue that he had no documentary source at all but wrote the narratives from oral tradition gathered from various people he spoke to. Given the strongly Semitic style of writing, though, both in the narratives and the 'canticles' (the songs of Zechariah, Mary and Simeon), which swiftly disappears in the rest of the Gospel, one can't help wondering whether he had a particularly Semitic source at hand while writing this part of the Gospel.

Unsurprisingly, scholars cannot agree on where this Semitic source might have come from, nor whether it might originally have been written in Aramaic or in Hebrew. This does suggest, however, that this part of Luke might originate from Palestinian Jewish Christian sources, which are different from the sources Luke used for the rest of his Gospel.

The Prophecy of John's Birth

Luke 1.5–25 In the days of King Herod of Judea, there was a priest named Zechariah, who belonged to the priestly order of Abijah. His wife was a descendant of Aaron, and her name was Elizabeth. [6]Both of them were righteous before God, living blamelessly according to all the commandments and regulations of the Lord. [7]But they had no children, because Elizabeth was barren, and both were getting on in years.

[8]Once when he was serving as priest before God and his section was on duty, [9]he was chosen by lot, according to the custom of the priesthood, to enter the sanctuary of the Lord and offer incense. [10]Now at the time of the incense offering, the whole assembly of the people was praying outside. [11]Then there appeared to him an angel of the Lord, standing at the right side of the altar of incense. [12]When Zechariah saw him, he was terrified; and fear overwhelmed him. [13]But the angel said to him, 'Do not be afraid, Zechariah, for your prayer has been heard. Your wife Elizabeth will bear you a son, and you will name him John. [14]You will have joy and gladness, and many will rejoice at his birth, [15]for he will be great in the sight of the Lord. He must never drink wine or strong drink; even before his birth he will be filled with the Holy Spirit. [16]He will turn many of the people of Israel to the Lord their God. [17]With the spirit and power of Elijah he will go before him, to turn the hearts of parents to their children, and the disobedient to the wisdom of the righteous, to make ready a people prepared for the Lord.' [18]Zechariah said to the angel, 'How will I know that this is so? For I am an old man, and my wife is getting on in years.' [19]The angel replied, 'I am Gabriel. I stand in the presence of God, and I have been sent to speak to you and to bring you this good news. [20]But now, because you did not believe my words, which will be fulfilled in their time, you will become mute, unable to speak, until the day these things occur.'

[21]Meanwhile the people were waiting for Zechariah, and wondered at his delay in the sanctuary. [22]When he did come out, he

> could not speak to them, and they realized that he had seen a vision in the sanctuary. He kept motioning to them and remained unable to speak. [23]When his time of service was ended, he went to his home.
>
> [24]After those days his wife Elizabeth conceived, and for five months she remained in seclusion. She said, [25] 'This is what the Lord has done for me when he looked favourably on me and took away the disgrace I have endured among my people.'

Fulfilment

Luke 1 can feel somewhat repetitive: the announcement to Zechariah followed by the announcement to Mary has a certain déjà vu feel to it. This is deliberate – the accounts carefully parallel each other. In each one God instigates the action (1.25; 1.30), the Holy Spirit plays a major part (1.15; 1.35) and God sends news of the action by Gabriel (1.19; 1.26). In some ways chapter 1 is a complete unit in itself. The theme of fulfilment runs all the way through it. It begins even in the prologue where Luke promised that Theophilus would see what has been fulfilled in our midst (1.1). It continues when Zechariah was told he would be unable to speak until Gabriel's words were fulfilled (1.20) and when Elizabeth blessed Mary for believing that what had been promised would be fulfilled (1.45).

Throughout chapter 1 fulfilment is both promised and attained. It is in itself a mini fulfilment narrative: God sent Gabriel to promise the birth of John (1.5–25), John was subsequently born (1.57–66) and Zechariah was able to speak again (1.67–80). In the middle of this narrative of fulfilment, Jesus' nd his future reign in God's kingdom is announced. There tle doubt that in this context we are expected to read n that the promises made to Mary will similarly be

Luke and Deuteronomy

One of the intriguing features of Luke's Gospel is that in certain ways it bears a remarkable similarity to Deuteronomy and the historical books, such as Joshua, 1 and 2 Samuel and 1 and 2 Kings – often called, as a collection, the Deuteronomistic Histories. This similarity can be observed in the grand way Luke tells his story, in the way the structure of Luke–Acts overlaps with the structure of the Elijah–Elisha story in 1 Kings 17.1—2 Kings 8.15, but possibly most clearly in Luke's interest in fulfilment in this chapter.

One of the strands that runs all the way through Deuteronomy and the historical books that follow is prophecy and fulfilment. Should you ever find yourself in need of a quiet afternoon's entertainment you could make a list of the promises God gives in these books and then tick them off when they are fulfilled. In case you do not have the time to do this, what you would discover is that every single promise made *is* fulfilled. My favourite obscure example of this is the prophecy given in Joshua 6.26 about the fate that awaited the person who attempted to rebuild Jericho:

Cursed before the Lord be anyone who tries
to build this city – this Jericho!
At the cost of his firstborn he shall lay its foundation,
and at the cost of his youngest he shall set up its gates!

Buried away in 1 Kings 16.34 is this:

In his days Hiel of Bethel built Jericho; he laid its foundation at the cost of Abiram his firstborn, and set up its gates at the cost of his youngest son Segub, according to the word of the Lord, which he spoke by Joshua son of Nun.

Luke seems to be signalling a similar theme of fulfilment of promise throughout this chapter. If promises are always fulfilled we pay more attention to the nature of the promise that is given.

An old, old story

The story of a barren couple who could not have children but were then given one by God occurs three times in the Old Testament. The announcement of John's birth is reminiscent of each of them in a different way. The three couples unable to conceive in the Old Testament were Abraham and Sarah (parents of Isaac); Manoah and his unnamed wife (parents of Samson) and Elkanah and Hannah (parents of Samuel).

In terms of style, the announcement of the birth of John feels closest to Judges 13.1–21. There an angel of the Lord appeared (Judges 13.3); the recipient of the vision was terrified (verse 6) and the angel announced the birth of the child and declared what characteristics he would have (verses 2–5). Mixed into that main narrative are additional details from the other two stories: a lack of belief that the prophecy would come true, which occurs when God announces the birth of Isaac to Sarah (Genesis 18.12), and the fact that the promise of the birth was made in the temple, as it was to Hannah (1 Samuel 1.17).

The main and somewhat intriguing difference between the announcement of John's birth and the announcement of the other three births – of Isaac, Samson and Samuel – is that in the Old Testament the primary recipient of the announcement was the mother, not as here the father. Having said that though, both Abraham and Manoah played a significant role in the story of the announcements of their sons' births.

These connections suggest that Luke intends us to draw to mind Abraham and Sarah, Manoah and his unnamed wife and Elkanah and Hannah in this passage. If this is the case then Luke may well be pointing us to the beginning of a new era. As with the birth of each of these characters, the fate of Israel was about to change and God's promises were about to come true. In each of these cases the giving of a child to a barren couple was about far more than that couple and that child. In each instance, the giving of the child symbolized God's intended intervention in the life of his people: in the case of Isaac to fulfil his promise to Abraham; in the case of Samson to save them from the Philistines; in the case of Samuel to save them from corruption and turning away from God. The prophecy of the birth of John, then, similarly prepares us not just for his birth but for God's intervention to save his people.

To complete the Old Testament underpinnings of this story, Luke also points us to Elijah. John was to be a new Elijah since he would the lead the people 'with the spirit and power of Elijah' (1.17). Just as Elijah fearlessly and uncompromisingly spoke power to power, regularly coming into conflict with Ahab and Jezebel, so John the Baptist would do the same, clashing with Herod Antipas and his wife Herodias. Just as Elijah time and time again called people back to God, so John the Baptist called people to repentance. This story is laced with clues from the Old Testament so that we understand more clearly how to view John the Baptist. As with so many stories in these opening chapters of Luke, what Luke tells us in this one resonates so powerfully with Old Testament narratives that we see the story with greater colour and depth.

And . . .

We noted above, when reflecting on Luke's sources, that the first two chapters of Luke are Semitic in style. One of the key features of Hebrew narrative is that, unlike Greek, it does not use many subordinate clauses but instead prefers to string together short sentences, often beginning with 'And . . .' or 'And it was . . .'. Even in English it is easy to see that they were used regularly in this narrative, which serves as an illustration of the contrast in style. In Luke 1.1–4, the elegant prologue, there is only one 'and'. In verses 5–25 (the passage we are looking at here) there are 18 'ands' – from verse 10 onwards they come at the start of almost every sentence, as they would in Hebrew.

---

* * *

Reflection

The effect of Luke's storytelling is to evoke a sense of a fracture in time. On one level it feels as though we have been here before many times. We are in the temple, there is a couple who cannot conceive, an angel appears and a child is foretold. This is a familiar story and it would not be out of place in certain parts of the Old Testament.

As the story unfolds, however, it becomes clear that in fact we have never been here before. Though there are familiar motifs and actions, the action of God that is about to break forth is like nothing we have ever seen before this point. Allowing the story to evoke an Old Testament context only reaffirms this point. This is an old, old story but also a brand new one. God is acting as he has on many occasions in the past *and* in new and entirely unexpected ways. As Luke's story unfolds, we observe this fracture in time ever widening until we recognize that this old, old story has changed the world for ever.

* * *

A priest named Zechariah

Luke opens his narrative of the announcement of John's birth by establishing the priestly credentials of John's parents. The Jewish priesthood was divided into 24 divisions (these divisions are outlined in 1 Chronicles 24.1–19). Apart from the three great festivals – Passover, Pentecost and Tabernacles – when all the priests were on duty, each division of priests served in the temple for two separate weeks each year. When they were not serving in the temple they lived in their home towns and villages. Due to their literacy, which was needed for the correct fulfilment of legal requirements, they were often leaders of their local communities and may even have been the 'scribes' mentioned so often in the Gospel accounts.

Priests did not have to marry daughters of priests – it would have been sufficient to marry someone of impeccable lineage – but priestly families were so revered and honoured that marriage between priestly families was not unusual. Luke begins his narrative, therefore, by establishing the purity of John's lineage – a priestly family on both sides.

Not only were Zechariah and Elizabeth genetically priests, they were also devout. This was clearly worth stressing. During the first century the priesthood came under attack for its corruption and self-interest. As a result a note stating the piety and religious devotion of those from a priestly line like Zechariah and Elizabeth would clear up any uncertainty about how respectable they were. Verse 6 maintained that both Zechariah and Elizabeth were *dikaioi* – the word used for 'righteous' in Greek – before the Lord *and* walked blamelessly according to the commandments. In other words they observed the law fully – the word 'walked' is often used of ethical expectations – but were also deemed to be 'righteous' before God. So they did not just 'do' the law mechanistically, it was written on their hearts and God deemed them righteous.

Luke's stress on the lineage and devotion to God of John's parents may well be intended to counteract the statement in verse 7 that they had no children. Barrenness was regularly interpreted as a sign of sin against God, so Luke's careful laying down of Zechariah's and Elizabeth's credentials seems to be to ensure that we do not make the mistake of assuming their childlessness had anything to do with their own actions. It is in some ways reminiscent, though much more implicit, of the conversation between Jesus and his disciples in John 9.2 about whether the man born blind had sinned or whether his parents had. There as here it is clear that no sin is attributed at all. There as here the miracle displays God's glory and reveals God's purpose.

The burning of incense

Zechariah's vision took place at the time of the burning of the incense. Twice each day a burnt offering was made in the temple, as a sign of devotion to God. The altar where the sacrifices took place stood directly in front of the temple building. In the morning before the burnt offering and in the evening after it, a priest would enter the temple building and burn incense to God just in front of the Holy of Holies. He would not have entered the Holy of Holies. Only a high priest could do that, and only then once a year on the Day of Atonement. The incense altar was the closest a priest who was not the high priest could get to the Holy of Holies – the place where God's glory was believed to dwell.

The large number of priests meant that someone might only have the chance to burn the incense once in their lifetime – hence Luke's comment that Zechariah was chosen by lot for this privilege. The task was so sought after that it was fairest to choose people by lot. The added significance of this is that the drawing of the Urim and Thummim from the high priest's breastplate – which was how lots were drawn in the temple – was regarded as revealing God's plan. So it was no coincidence that Zechariah found himself just outside the Holy of Holies when the angel of the Lord appeared.

Fear

One of the markers of a divine appearance in the Bible is fear. Both in the Old and the New Testaments fear is shown either in the presence of God (such as in Isaiah 6.5) or in the presence of an angel (Daniel 8.17). The response of fear is seen to be natural and right. God's holiness is so overwhelming that the correct response in God's presence is reverence and fear. The Greek word *phobos*, translated as 'fear', has a resonance not only of terror but of honour, awe and reverence: in short, fear is the recognition of the nature of God and of his 'otherness'.

The word *phobos* in Greek is the natural response to the appearance of God. In Luke this is not the only word used to describe a response to the angels. In Luke 1.12 not only does *phobos* fall on Zechariah, the verb *tarassō* is also used to describe his response. You might be interested to know that a similar verb, *diatarassō*, also described Mary's response to the arrival of Gabriel in 1.29. Intriguingly, although the NRSV translates *tarassō* as 'terrified' (in contrast to the NIV's 'startled' and the ESV's 'troubled'), the NRSV renders Mary's emotion as 'much perplexed' (in contrast to the 'greatly troubled' of the NIV and the ESV). The verb *tarassō* has a resonance of being tossed about, stirred up or thrown into confusion. Luke is stressing here that the arrival of an angel indicates that nothing will ever be the same again – no wonder they were terrified.

It is also worth noticing that fear in the presence of God also stretches to the presence of angels. Just as angels, like God, exude light and wear white garments, they also bring intimations of divine presence. Indeed in 1.19 Gabriel states clearly that he stands in the presence of God. As a result he did more than just bring messages, he also communicated God. So in the Bible human beings rightly react to angels in the same way they reacted to the presence of God.

Angels always start their message with the formulaic 'Do not be afraid'. It is important to notice that this is not because the person ought not to be afraid – fear and awe is an appropriate response to God's presence. The command not to fear comes so that the recipient of the message can go on to hear the rest of the angel's message. It also reassures them that though they are right to fear God, in this instance no harm will come to them.

Many will rejoice at his birth

In our modern world it is easy to forget that God's blessing is not just felt individually. A modern telling of this story might focus almost entirely on the joy felt by Zechariah and Elizabeth at the news of their forthcoming child. Luke does not diminish this expected joy in any way. Gabriel promised to Zechariah that his news would bring great joy. The phrase 'joy and gladness' (Luke 1.14), which is the usual translation of *chara* and *agalliasis*, does

However, the whole story suggests that we should not place too much emphasis on the punishment element of Zechariah's inability to speak. The offering of a sign as a marker that the promise would be fulfilled is commonplace in the Old Testament: a smoking furnace and burning lamp passed between Abraham's sacrifice as a sign of God's promise to him (Genesis 17.6–17); Moses' staff became a serpent as a sign in Exodus 4.1–3; Ahaz was given a sign – even though he refused to ask for one – in Isaiah 7.10–17. Signs prove the veracity of the message given. Zechariah too is given a sign, and it seems as though the fact that it was a sign is far more important than any implication of punishment.

The impact of this sign is that Zechariah was not able to pre-empt the proclamation of the good news until John was actually born.

Gabriel

Since this is the first, though not the last time that Gabriel appears in Luke's narrative, it is worth noting a few things about him. Angels were not named until relatively late in the Old Testament tradition. The book of Daniel is the place where we first encounter both specific jobs and names for some key angels. Until then they were just termed 'the angel of the Lord'. In Jewish texts of the Second Temple period, speculation about angels became more and more elaborate until there were extensive rankings of them and seven archangels were identified and named. Gabriel was one of those seven, alongside Michael (also mentioned in the Bible – Daniel 12.1; Jude 1.9; Revelation 12.7), Raphael (who appears in Tobit), Uriel, Raguel, Remiel and Saraqael.

Gabriel appears most commonly as a messenger angel, as here. It is worth noting that the names of all these archangels end with '-el', the Hebrew word for God, because the name of God is in them.

---

* * *

The prophecy of John's birth feels very much like a story from the Old Testament – it would not seem much out of place in Judges or 1 Samuel. As with the genealogy, Luke is reminding us here that this story he is telling is not just a brand new narrative, falling into the world in a way never experienced before. Rather this is a story of ancient origins, one that picks up again the threads of the Old Testament and reminds us that God's people have been waiting for someone to come and transform their lives for centuries.

In one way the birth of John is nothing new. Countless previous heroes have been born to save their people. They have even been born in very similar circumstances: to barren parents, with promises given by angels and vows to live a holy life. Seen in this way, then, this really is an old, old story. God's message has come again that he will act to save his people. A new hero will arise who will turn God's people back to each other as well as back to God (see 1.17).

What makes this story radically different though is that, unlike all previous narratives, it doesn't end here – or even with the birth and life of the hero about to be born. The whole point of Luke 1 is that it is preparation. We know John will be born as Gabriel has promised. We know he will grow up to be the person Gabriel said he would be. Fulfilment *will* take place but this time John is not the sole point of the story. John's success as a priestly prophet who will turn the people back to each other and to God is in itself only preparation for the real story.

John's calling is like so many others in the Old Testament and like none of them. John functioned simply as the one who would prepare God's people for God himself, born as a baby among us. It is worth reminding ourselves of this time after time. It is easy to slip into the assumption that the revelation of God in the world is entirely down to us; that the success or failure of God's kingdom breaking in rests entirely on our shoulders. The reality is that we are called to be like John – not to be Jesus. We are called to turn people back to each other and back to God so that when they see Jesus they can recognize him to be who he is. We, like John, are called to be the warm-up acts and nothing more.

4

The Prophecy of Jesus' Birth

The Prophecy to Mary

On one level the prophecy of Jesus' birth seems oddly located, slipped in the middle of the much longer story of the prophecy and then fulfilment of John's birth. As we noticed above, however, this is for a very good reason. The longer story of John's birth gives us the lens through which we read this story of the prophecy of Jesus' birth. One of Luke's favourite literary devices is to wrap one narrative up in another so that you see the central one in a new light. This is certainly the case here. Wrapping the prophecy of Jesus' birth in the prophecy of John's means that certain details spring to the eye more clearly. For example, Mary's connection to the house of David is more striking once we have already reflected on John's connection to the priestly line, and Mary's inability to have children – because she was a young girl and not yet married – is brought to the fore by Zechariah's and Elizabeth's barrenness. Luke has already prepared us for this prophecy; he has trained our eyes so that we can see it in more detail.

Luke 1.26–38   In the sixth month the angel Gabriel was sent by God to a town in Galilee called Nazareth, [27]to a virgin engaged to a man whose name was Joseph, of the house of David. The virgin's name was Mary. [28]And he came to her and said, 'Greetings, favoured one! The Lord is with you.' [29]But she was much perplexed by his words and pondered what sort of greeting this might be. [30]The angel said to her, 'Do not be afraid, Mary, for you have found favour with God. [31]And now, you will conceive in your

---

womb and bear a son, and you will name him Jesus. [32]He will be great, and will be called the Son of the Most High, and the Lord God will give to him the throne of his ancestor David. [33]He will reign over the house of Jacob for ever, and of his kingdom there will be no end.' [34]Mary said to the angel, 'How can this be, since I am a virgin?' [35]The angel said to her, 'The Holy Spirit will come upon you, and the power of the Most High will overshadow you; therefore the child to be born will be holy; he will be called Son of God. [36]And now, your relative Elizabeth in her old age has also conceived a son; and this is the sixth month for her who was said to be barren. [37]For nothing will be impossible with God.' [38]Then Mary said, 'Here am I, the servant of the Lord; let it be with me according to your word.' Then the angel departed from her.

Setting the scene

The story of the prophecy of John's birth took place in Jerusalem at the temple. Although Zechariah went home following that prophecy, Luke does not tell us where his home was. In verse 39 we see Mary travelling to an unnamed town in 'the hill country of Judea' to visit Elizabeth. The hill country of Judea stretches for around 45 miles between Samaria and the Negev desert in the south. In Christian tradition the traditional location for John's birth was Ein Kerem on the south-west outskirts of Jerusalem, but there is little evidence that allows us to be confident of this location.

In contrast Luke is very clear about the place where Mary received a visit from Gabriel. At the time of the prophecy Mary lived in Nazareth, which is 15 miles west of the southern end of the Sea of Galilee. At this time Nazareth was an obscure agricultural village and, apart from in the New Testament, not mentioned in literature at all until about the third century AD. Nor was it on any trade route and, with a population of about 450, was a very small village. Its location and obscurity explain why, as an adult, Jesus moved to

Capernaum on the northern coast of Galilee, located on the main trade route east to west from the Mediterranean ports. If he had remained in Nazareth it is unlikely anyone outside of the 450 who lived in the village would have heard of him.

Matthew and Nazareth

One of the key differences often observed between Matthew's birth narratives and those of Luke is that Luke locates Mary in Nazareth before Jesus' birth, only travelling to Bethlehem at the time of the birth. Matthew, in contrast, makes no mention at all of Nazareth until Joseph and Mary returned from exile in Egypt, when they then settled in Nazareth. Of course this does not rule out the possibility of Mary living there before Jesus' birth but there is no evidence that Matthew was aware of this tradition.

Possibly more important than this difference is the tradition that both Gospel writers hold in common: that Jesus was born in Bethlehem but grew up in Nazareth. Luke attributes the growing up in Nazareth to its being where Mary and Joseph lived; Matthew to their settling there after their exile.

Luke sets Gabriel's visit to Mary six months into Elizabeth's pregnancy, though what significance we are to draw from this – other than that the pregnancies overlapped – is hard to discern. It is possible that Luke is pointing to the fact that, though becoming significant before Jesus, John was of a very similar age and that the moment of God's intervention in the world had begun at the same time. It is also possible that the timing described by Luke was intended to indicate that Mary was unaware of Elizabeth's pregnancy. If John could not speak and Elizabeth went into seclusion for five months after his return (1.24), then Mary would not have known about Elizabeth's pregnancy until it was announced to her by Gabriel in verse 36. Perhaps her visit, then, in verse 39 was a means of verifying all she had been told by Gabriel in his visit.

A *virgin whose name was Mary*

There is much to reflect on in the statements about Mary's virginity and we will take each issue as it occurs in each of the texts. Here the issue is simply the word *parthenos*, used to describe Mary in verse 27.

Luke, like Matthew, stressed the point that Mary was a virgin. In fact if anything, Luke stressed Mary's virginity more than Matthew. In Matthew 1.23 it was included largely through a quotation from Isaiah 7.14 – which we will explore more below – and a reference to Joseph's having no marital relations with her before Jesus was born (1.25). Luke stresses Mary's virginity twice – once in a general description of Mary (1.27, where the word is used twice) and once from Mary's own lips when she wondered how the conception was possible (1.34).

On one level Mary's virginity is entirely unremarkable. The Greek word used of Mary is *parthenos*. This simply refers to a young girl of marriageable age who, by virtue of not yet being married, was a virgin. As we shall see below when we explore Isaiah 7.14, *parthenos* has a more explicit meaning of 'virgin' than the Hebrew equivalent *'almah*, which has more of an emphasis of 'young woman'. Indeed Luke emphasizes the explicit 'virginal' element of the word in 1.34 when Mary says, 'How can this be, since I am a virgin?'

In Roman law of the time, the minimum age for marriage for girls was 12 and for boys 14 (with an additional minimum betrothal age of 10). Jewish marriage custom was very similar to this. A girl was normally married by the time she was twelve and a half years old. This was designed as a way of guaranteeing the virginity of the girl when she was married, by ensuring she was married by the start of puberty. In a world in which child mortality was high, it also guaranteed the longest possible childbearing period for the girl.

Before the first century BC, betrothal was not normally distinguished significantly from marriage. Marriage was constituted by the drawing up of a deed, the exchange of money with the groom and sexual intercourse. Betrothal involved the first two of these but not the third. It was as binding as marriage

and, after betrothal, the couple could only be separated by
death or divorce. There were normally twelve months between
betrothal and marriage, in which the young girl would stay at
her father's house until she was old enough for marriage. This
pinpoints the age of Mary in this encounter quite precisely.
If she was betrothed but not married she would probably be
somewhere between the age of 11 and 12.

Mary was engaged to Joseph

Modern translations of both Luke 1.27 and Matthew 1.18 often
opt for the translation that says Mary was engaged to Joseph.
This raises fascinating questions about meaning. The problem
is that we no longer have a modern word that captures the full
legal meaning of the word 'betrothal'. 'Engaged' implies a pre-
liminary arrangement prior to the full marriage ceremony but
not the expectation that it was the first stage of marriage. The
(unsolvable) question is whether it is better to use a word that
means something to us even if it doesn't capture the entirety of
'betrothal' or use a word that no longer really means anything but
where the explanation of what it *does* mean can identify what is
going on in the text.

---

* * *

Reflection

The lengthy discussions about the nature of Mary's virginity
can distract us from a central part of this narrative. While it
is remarkable and worthy of deep reflection that a virgin might
conceive a child, if we charge on from here with ever more elaborate doctrinal discussions about the virgin birth we run the risk
of missing another key feature of the narrative – the age of Mary.

Our mental pictures of Mary, aided it must be said by centuries of Christian art, place her in her late teens or early twenties. Even at that age she would be young – by our standards – for facing the consequences of Gabriel's message to her. The scandal, potential abuse and destruction of her reputation were guaranteed by being pregnant while betrothed but not married. Even if the baby were Joseph's, Mary's reputation would be in tatters, but to bear the news that she was pregnant and not by her betrothed would have led to certain disgrace.

Now add to that picture that the girl we are talking about was probably no older than 13, and more likely 11 to 12. If she had been older, comment would surely have been made by Luke, not least because, culturally, it would have been harder to guarantee her virginity. So we are challenged here to remove from our mental art gallery the older woman and replace her, instead, with a pre-teen.

This is where the challenge occurs. For me, particularly because I am a mother with a teenage and a pre-teen daughter, the unsettling question that emerges here is focused on Mary's age. Here is a young girl who, as far as Luke's account records, is asked by God to face disgrace in order to bring salvation into the world. She is charged with facing that disgrace – and potential danger to life and limb – alone, and she does it with courage and dignity.

The mother in me rails at God for asking too much of a young girl, but the Christian marvels at the courage of this young girl, Mary, whose sacrifice of her own reputation and safety enabled The Word made flesh, God with us, to be born in our midst.

* * *

Greetings favoured one!

A small and insignificant detail in the Greek of Luke 1.28 sets the scene for Gabriel's greeting to Mary: Luke indicates that the meeting between Mary and Gabriel took place indoors. The Greek word used is *eiselthōn*, which means literally 'coming into'. There are many caves around lower Galilee and there is a particular concentration of them in Nazareth. Archaeological evidence suggests that these were inhabited, even at the time of Jesus. There is a good chance Mary dwelt in one of these caves and it is possible, therefore, that our mental picture of these events needs to include not a house but a cave, into which Gabriel went to deliver his message from God.

Some phrases of the New Testament have been the subject of huge discussion, speculation and theological dispute, and none more so than the greeting by the angel to Mary, *chaire kecharitōmenē*. The dispute arises not from the Greek words but from the Latin translation of them. The first word is straightforward: *chaire* means simply 'greetings' and is the usual way to greet someone when you meet them. Alongside this the word also means rejoice and may therefore suggest a theological 'act and response': God acts towards his people with grace and they respond with joy. In other words it is possible that this phrase might also be translated 'Rejoice, favoured one' and that within it is the suggestion that Mary's response to God's gracious favour should be one of joy.

This, of course, has not been what has caused such dispute; it is the Latin translation that did that. The Latin translation of the phrase is *ave gratia plena*. Where the Greek means that Mary has had grace bestowed upon her, the Latin can also mean that she was in a state of having been filled with grace; that is, before her meeting with Gabriel, hence the phrase is often rendered 'full of grace' in English. Catholic tradition understands this to mean that she was in a state of perpetual favour. The nub of the argument is whether Mary is to be seen as permanently favoured by God from before her own birth, or the recipient of grace simply from the moment of the angel's greeting.

The third part of Gabriel's greeting in Luke should not be overlooked: 'the Lord is with you'. Mary was, rightly, greatly troubled by Gabriel's greeting – the assurance that someone is favoured by God *should* trouble them. All the way through the Bible, with great favour from God comes great responsibility.

Being assured of God's favour feels a little like the two-edged wish of the Chinese proverb, 'May you live in interesting times'. Being favoured by God means that your life is about to be turned on its head.

This is where the third element of Gabriel's wish becomes important. God did favour Mary and did ask of her an almost unbearable task, but at the same time promised to be with her through it all. He accompanied her along the way and made the undoable doable.

Blessed art thou among women

Those who know their KJV may be surprised in modern translations by the omission of the phrase 'Blessed art thou among women'. This phrase was present in the Greek text used by the translators of the KJV but is not present in modern Greek New Testament texts. This is because it is not in the most reliable manuscripts and appears to have been misplaced from Luke 1.42, when Elizabeth says this precise phrase to Mary.

This misplacement may have arisen from its use in the Hail Mary – 'Hail Mary, full of grace, the Lord is with thee, Blessed art thou among women' – and have been added here accidentally by a later scribe.

Gabriel's announcement of Jesus' birth to Mary mirrors other Old Testament texts in which the birth of a son is announced – see for example Judges 13.3–5. Somewhat intriguingly, however, it is closest to Genesis 16.11, which is the encounter between Hagar and an angel in the wilderness. Hagar was pregnant and Sarah had treated her so badly that she had run away. The angel said to her, 'Now you have conceived and shall bear a son; you shall call him Ishmael' and then went on to describe what he would do as a man. The wording is very similar here and calls to mind yet another occasion in the history of the people of God when God intervened to save them through an unlikely woman in unexpected circumstances.

How can this be?

As we noted above, the contrast between the angel's response to Zechariah's question ('How will I know that this is so?) and Mary's ('How can this be?') seems a little harsh. In the one case Zechariah is punished by being rendered unable to speak and in the other Mary is given a simple explanation of how this can be. Again, as we noted above, the clue seems to be in recognizing the importance of signs. Zechariah's inability to speak was a sign to him of the veracity of the message; Elizabeth's pregnancy was a sign to Mary of the veracity of her message. The outcome of the conversation seems to be much more about demonstrating the truth of what has been said than about punishment. If there is an element of punishment implied it must be for a tone of voice that is no longer captured in the text.

Mary's question allows Gabriel to make explicit what has previously been implicit: that the conception of Jesus is by the agency of the Holy Spirit, making him the Son of God in more than just name. It also allows an unequivocal statement from the lips of Mary that she was genuinely a virgin (and not just a young girl). It is interesting that the majority of modern translations have gone with the more euphemistic 'since I am a virgin' translation of the Greek. Mary's statement is much grittier than that and was literally 'since I do not know a man'. Here 'know' is used in the Old Testament sense of intercourse and thus is a declaration not so much about status as about actions – or lack of them.

The virgin birth

It is worth at this point pausing to clarify terms. I am regularly asked by people whether I believe in the virgin birth. The answer is 'No I do not', but this doesn't mean what some might assume. I believe in the virginal conception of Jesus but not the virgin birth. This may seem to be an overly picky point but it is an important one. The virgin birth when used technically within Catholic theology is the dogma that Mary was

---

a virgin before, during and after the conception and birth of Jesus.

This is not a doctrine I hold nor is it suggested to me by the biblical texts. The birth narratives do not suggest that Jesus was born in anything other than the normal way, and I take the references to his brothers as just that: references to Jesus' siblings. Nevertheless it is worth noting that the perpetual virginity of Mary was widely held as a doctrine by the fourth century AD and has been influential in Catholic theology ever since. It was also supported by key Protestant figures like Martin Luther (for more on the virgin birth see pp. 95–6 below).

* * *

Reflection

Discussions about the virginal conception of Jesus illustrate in microcosm the bigger questions about historicity and veracity that circle the stories of Jesus' birth. Those for and against the historicity of the virginal conception of Jesus can trade evidence and lack of evidence backwards and forward, but the harsh truth remains that we do not, and maybe could not, have the necessary evidence to demonstrate its truth to those who do not accept Jesus' virginal conception, nor do we have evidence in the opposite direction that will undermine once and for all the beliefs of those who do accept it.

For those who have been engaging with these arguments for many years it can feel a little as though you are on a carousel going round and round, up and down, the same music playing – making no discernible progress forward.

The reality is that we need to accept the point we explored briefly in the Introduction, namely that the case put forward for the virginal conception of Jesus by the Gospel writers was designed to persuade a first-century not a twenty-first-century audience. The best we can do is ask the question about what they were attempting to convince their audience of and to see what more we gain from the stories as a result.

The strong ties to the Old Testament tradition suggested both in Gabriel's wording to Mary at Luke 1.31 – 'You will conceive in your womb and bear a son' – and in the wrap-around story of the birth of John the Baptist remind us of God's presence at key points in his people's history: intervening, shaping and saving those he loved. Just as he intervened to give Abraham a son and to provide leaders like Samson and Samuel, so again God was intervening in history to remind the people that the Lord was with them. This time, however, the Lord was with them in a way far more profound than ever before.

It is possible, as some suggest, that Jesus' divine conception was written into the tradition as a means of combating the stories about the divine conception of people like Alexander the Great, the Roman general Scipio Africanus and Octavian (later known as the Emperor Augustus), but the emphasis of these other stories is quite different. The tradition about Augustus' birth was that his mother Atia was serving the God Apollo in the temple. In her sleep a serpent glided up to her and then went away. Since then a mark of the serpent was to be seen on her body and in the tenth month after this a baby was born. The story was designed to communicate Octavian's future importance, but nothing more.

In my view the purpose of Matthew and Luke's accounts of the virginal conception is very different. These accounts are their version of John's beautiful and poetic statement that God became truly human and dwelt among us. They contain the same point differently expressed. Both are mysterious in different ways. Just as I do not seek to understand precisely how it was possible for the divine Word to exist from the dawn of time, so I also do not seek to understand the nature of divine conception. They are beyond my comprehension. In the prophecy of Jesus' birth Luke introduces us, in his way, to the mystery of the incarnation, and for me at least, that is sufficient.

* * *

Mary's Visit to Elizabeth

The whole of the first chapter of Luke drives us to the meeting of Mary and Elizabeth. It is the linchpin of all the stories we have explored so far. It may not be the most exciting in terms of narrative but it is the very heart of Luke's story. Here the stories of Mary and Elizabeth intertwine physically as well as symbolically. Here what has been promised to both women is confirmed. Here Mary's true response to Gabriel's message – beyond the rather stilted 'let it be with me according to your word' – is proclaimed and heard. Here we understand that the action of God evokes response, and a response beyond all human imagining.

In her meeting with Elizabeth, Mary received a double sign of the truth of what Gabriel had announced to her. The first was that Elizabeth was pregnant as Gabriel had said she would be. Luke's timings dictate that at six-months pregnant she would have been clearly and visibly pregnant. The second sign was given verbally to Mary by Elizabeth, who recognized that she was bearing a child and pronounced a blessing both on Mary and on the child in her womb.

Luke's description of John's greeting of Jesus is a delightful one. Several commentators observe that the oriental greeting was an extended affair. In other words Mary on this occasion did not simply say 'Hello', but would have made a formal and quite lengthy address. In the middle of this the baby in Elizabeth's womb leapt in recognition of the baby in Mary's. One of Luke's great themes that runs throughout his Gospel is that of recognition of who Jesus really was. The model for this recognition is offered to us by John: before he could see, hear or meet him himself, he recognized Jesus for who he was and leapt with the joy of the recognition.

Elizabeth's response to Mary is equally delightful. In verse 42 and again in verse 45 she declared the blessed state of Mary and the child she carried. The verb used in verse 42 is *eulogeō*, which can be used to pray for God's blessing on someone. In this instance, however, it is, like the words of Gabriel, recognition of already existing blessing. Mary and the fruit of her womb are to be recognized as blessed. In the second blessing in verse 45 the word for blessing changes – here it is *makarios*, the word used by Jesus in the beatitudes, perhaps suggesting that in Mary we should recognize a true child of God that Jesus talked about there.

The Magnificat

Luke 1.39–56 In those days Mary set out and went with haste to a Judean town in the hill country, [40]where she entered the house of Zechariah and greeted Elizabeth. [41]When Elizabeth heard Mary's greeting, the child leapt in her womb. And Elizabeth was filled with the Holy Spirit [42]and exclaimed with a loud cry, 'Blessed are you among women, and blessed is the fruit of your womb. [43]And why has this happened to me, that the mother of my Lord comes to me? [44]For as soon as I heard the sound of your greeting, the child in my womb leapt for joy. [45]And blessed is she who believed that there would be a fulfilment of what was spoken to her by the Lord.'

[46]And Mary said,

'My soul magnifies the Lord,
[47]and my spirit rejoices in God my Saviour,
[48]for he has looked with favour on the lowliness of his servant.
Surely, from now on all generations will call me blessed;
[49]for the Mighty One has done great things for me, and holy is his name.
[50]His mercy is for those who fear him from generation to generation. [51]He has shown strength with his arm;
he has scattered the proud in the thoughts of their hearts.
[52]He has brought down the powerful from their thrones,
and lifted up the lowly;
[53]he has filled the hungry with good things,
and sent the rich away empty.
[54]He has helped his servant Israel,
in remembrance of his mercy,
[55]according to the promise he made to our ancestors,
to Abraham and to his descendants for ever.'

> [56]And Mary remained with her for about three months and then returned to her home.

Just as it is hard to talk about John 1.1–18, it is also hard to talk about Mary's song, the Magnificat. It is so well known, well loved and well used that it is almost impossible to say anything more of any value about it. It would, however, be wrong not to try, so what follows, though inevitably missing much of importance, will attempt to reflect on something of the power of Mary's song.

Luke's canticles

One of the striking features of Luke's birth narratives from this point on is that they are punctuated with what are commonly known as canticles or songs of praise. Each of them has become significant in the worship life of the Church, and they are commonly known by the Latin word or words with which they begin: the Magnificat (Mary's song from Luke 1.46–55); the Benedictus (Zechariah's song from 1.68–79); the Gloria (the angels' song from 2.14); the Nunc Dimittis (Simeon's song from 2.29–32).

There is much discussion about the origins of these songs. Suggestions include that Luke wrote them at the same time as the rest of the Gospel; that he wrote them later and added them in; that he used pre-existing songs of Jewish or Christian origin, which he inserted into his text. One of the questions here is how integral to the narrative each of the songs feels. Some scholars are of the view that you could remove them entirely from the text with little impact on the surrounding material; others consider them more crucial to the story. My own feeling is that the narrative would be very much poorer without something like the canticles – even if they were much shorter – and that something like them is necessary within Luke's theology to express a response to God's goodness. If we need something *like* the canticles in Luke then why not propose the canticles themselves?

Another point to consider is the fact that the canticles are themselves very Hebraic in character. They have a Hebraic style and draw upon many Old Testament themes – in fact so much so that they would feel very much at home in the Psalter or tucked elsewhere in one of the historical books. Given that Luke's birth narratives are also characteristically Hebraic in style, this suggests that the canticles might have been found in whatever source Luke used to construct this part of his narrative.

The Magnificat and the Old Testament

The Magnificat is full of Old Testament references and allusions. Probably the most important of all is its parallel with Hannah's song from 1 Samuel 2.1–10. In fact the two songs are so close that it is worth looking at them side by side.

Hannah's song (1 Samuel 2.1-10)	Mary's song (Luke 1.46-55)
Hannah prayed and said, 'My heart exults in the Lord; my strength is exalted in my God. My mouth derides my enemies, because I rejoice in my victory.	And Mary said, 'My soul magnifies the Lord, [47]and my spirit rejoices in God my Saviour, [48]for he has looked with favour on the lowliness of his servant. Surely, from now on all generations will call me blessed;
[2]There is no Holy One like the Lord, no one besides you; there is no Rock like our God.	[49]for the Mighty One has done great things for me, and holy is his name. [50]His mercy is for those who fear him from generation to generation.
[3]Talk no more so very proudly, let not arrogance come from your mouth; for the Lord is a God of knowledge, and by him actions are weighed. [4]The bows of the mighty are broken, but the feeble gird on strength.	[51]He has shown strength with his arm; he has scattered the proud in the thoughts of their hearts. [52]He has brought down the powerful from their thrones, and lifted up the lowly;

⁵Those who were full have hired themselves out for bread, but those who were hungry are fat with spoil. The barren has borne seven, but she who has many children is forlorn. ⁶The Lord kills and brings to life; he brings down to Sheol and raises up. ⁷The Lord makes poor and makes rich; he brings low, he also exalts. ⁸He raises up the poor from the dust; he lifts the needy from the ash heap, to make them sit with princes and inherit a seat of honour. For the pillars of the earth are the Lord's, and on them he has set the world. ⁹He will guard the feet of his faithful ones, but the wicked shall be cut off in darkness; for not by might does one prevail. ¹⁰The Lord! His adversaries shall be shattered; the Most High will thunder in heaven. The Lord will judge the ends of the earth; he will give strength to his king, and exalt the power of his anointed.'	⁵³he has filled the hungry with good things, and sent the rich away empty.
	⁵⁴He has helped his servant Israel, in remembrance of his mercy, ⁵⁵according to the promise he made to our ancestors, to Abraham and to his descendants for ever.'

There are many points of contact between the two songs: both begin in praise of God for what he has done for them; they then move on to statements about God's might (he is a rock in Hannah's song and a mighty one in Mary's); the next section talks about the grand subversion of God, undermining the power of the rich and wealthy and lifting up those with no status or power.

Mary's song alone ends with turning to Israel and what God has done for the nation as a whole. Indeed the end of her song gives it a balance Hannah's does not have in the same way. Mary's falls into two halves, each of which contains the repetition of 'his servant' (1.48, 54); 'the mercy of God' (1.48, 50, 54); 'the lowly' (1.48, 52) and a recognition of the perpetuity of God's mercy (1.50, 55). As a result the song moves from the personal (1.46–50) to the corporate (1.51–55) in recognition that God's mercy to her affects far more than just Mary herself. God's mercy stretches outwards from Mary to encompass the rest of his people – and then later the whole world.

It is features like this that undermine the claim of some that the Magnificat is 'just' a rehash of Hannah's song. There can be no doubt that Hannah's song stands in the background of Mary's, but Mary's song is much more than Hannah's: Hannah's is simply a song of personal salvation; Mary's is a recognition of national salvation in the light of the mercy shown to her personally. It is this movement from personal to global that, in fact, has made the Magnificat so well loved and well used throughout Christian history. There is something profound about the recognition that individual redemption brings corporate redemption and vice versa. Mary's song is very much not just about Mary, and this is why we can all sing it with such heartfelt meaning.

It is also worth noting that Hannah's song is not the only Old Testament resonance in the Magnificat – indeed the Magnificat is widely acknowledged to be a collage of Old Testament texts. The list below will give you a flavour of how extensive the Old Testament background is:

- **Genesis 30.13** And Leah said, 'Happy am I! For the women will call me happy'; so she named him Asher.
- **Deuteronomy 10.21** He is your praise; he is your God, who has done for you these great and awesome things that your own eyes have seen.
- **Psalm 111.9** Holy and awesome is his name.
- **Psalm 103.17** But the steadfast love of the Lord is from everlasting to everlasting on those who fear him, and his righteousness to children's children.

- **Job 40.12** Look on all who are proud, and bring them low; tread down the wicked where they stand.
- **Psalm 98.3** He has remembered his steadfast love and faithfulness to the house of Israel. All the ends of the earth have seen the victory of our God.

These are just a few of the many allusions to Old Testament narratives and texts that can be found in the Magnificat. The list could go on for a few pages.

As a result it is hard to maintain that the Magnificat is merely a rehash of Old Testament texts. Instead it indicates that it is a deep and profound praying again of those texts of praise and wonder in the light of the new events unfolding. Indeed its similarity to the Old Testament songs of praise, including the Psalms, might give us an insight into how the Psalms were used in daily prayer and worship. Rather than being simply read again as we do, it is possible that the Psalms were used as a spiritual treasury from which structure, phrases and even whole sections were drawn in order to express lament, praise or thanksgiving about what was happening at the time. The Magnificat could well be a living example of how the Psalms and other Old Testament songs were used in the first century.

God as divine warrior and bearer of mercy

One of the striking features of the Magnificat is that there are two main – and strikingly contrasting – depictions of God given throughout it. On the one hand God is described as a divine warrior: he is mighty (1.49); shows strength (51); scatters the proud (51); brings down the powerful (52). Interwoven with these descriptions are accounts of God's tender care and mercy: he has looked with favour (48); his name is holy (49); he has mercy on those that fear him (50); he has lifted up the lowly (52); filled the hungry (53); helped Israel (54). The two go together hand in hand. God's might is what makes space for his mercy. His defence of the lowly inevitably leads to the toppling of the powerful. His bringing down of this earth's rulers is what makes a different rule possible. You cannot have one without the other. God's mercy is dependent entirely upon his ability to bring down the powerful – without that his mercy would have little impact or use.

How do we make God greater?

One of the odd features of Hebrew praise is the language used. We are often exhorted to 'give glory to God' or to 'glorify him' – Psalm 115.1 for example – and here Mary declares that she will magnify God, in other words enlarge or make greater. This raises some intriguing questions. How is it possible to make God any greater than he already is? How is it possible to give God any more glory than he already has?

The answer lies in relationship rather than absolute state. God is great and remains great whether we worship him or not. He is glorious and remains glorious whether we recognize that or not. We do not change God's state when we worship him. Instead we change both our relationship with him and his repute in the world. Mary's statement that she 'enlarged God' was a statement about God's importance in her own life and estimation, not an absolute statement about who God was. Our calling in worship is constantly to be seeking to make God's impact on our lives greater and more significant, and the impact of other things smaller and less significant. In a sense Mary's opening phrase 'My soul magnifies the Lord' reminds us powerfully of what worship is all about.

Mary's song, with its deep steeping in Scripture, reminds us that God's action to Mary – and hence to his people in Israel – was not a one-off. Mary was not just expressing who God was once but who God is and therefore who God will always be.

Reflection

One of the reasons why the Magnificat remains such a powerful song is because it is a near perfect example of worship. It begins with Mary placing herself in relationship to God and stating her intention to make God as great as possible in her life, before moving on to recount the reasons why she will do this. Using words, phrases and ideas from the whole of Scripture she laid out God's nature as one who defends the weak and combats the powerful so that he could demonstrate his eternal mercy, his ongoing care and compassion from generation to generation.

Mary did not stop there – she recognized that God's mercy to her was not just personal. Hers was not just an individual experience. The impact of God's mercy would transform the place where she lived. Not only would her life never be the same again but Israel's life would be transformed too.

This movement to place God in the centre of our lives and to make him as great as possible, to remember all the good things God has done not only for us but for the whole world, lies at the heart of worship. That movement from us to God, from God to the world around us, gives us the perfect model for worship and is one of the reasons why the Magnificat remains one of the best loved songs in the whole Bible.

* * *

The Prophecy to Joseph

Matthew 1.18–23   Now the birth of Jesus the Messiah took place in this way. When his mother Mary had been engaged to Joseph, but before they lived together, she was found to be with child from the Holy Spirit. [19]Her husband Joseph, being a righteous man and unwilling to expose her to public disgrace, planned to dismiss her quietly. [20]But just when he had resolved to do this, an angel of the Lord appeared to him in a dream and said, 'Joseph, son of David, do not be afraid to take Mary as your wife, for the child conceived in her is from the Holy Spirit. [21]She will bear a son, and you are to name him Jesus, for he will save his people from their sins.' [22]All this took place to fulfil what had been spoken by the Lord through the prophet: [23]'Look, the virgin shall conceive and bear a son, and they shall name him Emmanuel', which means, 'God is with us.'

It may seem an odd thing to say, but Matthew does not really have a birth narrative. Despite the grand title in 1.18 that 'the birth of Jesus the Messiah took place in this way', Matthew does not really tell us the details of precisely which way the birth took place. Like Luke he places emphasis on the circumstances surrounding the conception of Jesus – and the announcement of that conception – but not on the birth itself. It is only the final two verses of this passage (vv. 24–25) that mention the birth at all. Chapter 2 of Matthew begins after the birth with the magi visiting Jesus. Strictly speaking, then, Matthew joins Mark and John in having no actual birth narratives. He has a prophecy of Jesus' birth and a visit after the birth, but no birth itself.

Joseph's story

Matthew, like Luke, identifies the conception of Jesus as taking place while Mary was betrothed but not married to Joseph (see the discussion of betrothal above, pp. 54–5). Matthew provides the same basic information as Luke but in a different way. In Luke, Mary states to Gabriel that she has never known a man; in Matthew it is emphasized that the events took place before she had left her own home and moved in with Joseph.

In other words Matthew makes it clear that the first two elements of marriage were in place – the drawing up of a legal deed and the exchange of the money – but the third element of living in the same house had not yet happened. The effect of the two accounts is the same, even though the details are told in a different way.

It is interesting to notice, though, that Matthew's attention is focused much more closely on Joseph's story than on Mary's. The slightly strange effect of this is that Mary fades into the background and is no more than a passive foil to Joseph. In great contrast to Luke, she has no voice and the description of the conception is as a result rather vague: literally the Greek says that 'she was found having in the womb from the Holy Spirit'. Some commentators observe that the phrase 'from the Holy Spirit' in verse 18 is so unclear – and only explained two verses later – that Matthew is assuming here that his readers already know the story and will understand what his slightly cryptic comment means.

Matthew is keen to show Joseph in a good light. What is unclear is what he means by describing Joseph as a 'righteous' or 'just' man (the Greek word used here is *dikaios*). Within Judaism, righteousness was demonstrated by fulfilling the requirements of the law. In this instance those requirements seem to demand that Joseph divorce Mary. There is considerable discussion about whether the word *kai* between 'being a just man' and 'unwilling to expose her to public disgrace' is better translated as 'but'. If translated as 'but', the sentence makes slightly more sense of the usual use of *dikaios* as 'to be righteous': He was a righteous man – and so had to divorce her – but didn't want to expose her publicly.

Slightly frustratingly, the practice of divorce in the first century is not clearly described. The bizarre and cruel things described in Numbers 5.11–31 (which seem akin to the medieval witch trials) that could be enacted by a man who suspected his wife of adultery but had no proof do not, thankfully, seem to have been widely practised. Instead divorce appears to have been more common, though the grounds upon which you could divorce your wife were heavily disputed and range from serious transgressions like adultery (Rabbi

Shammai) to trivial reasons such as burning a meal (Rabbi Hillel).
Joseph's grounds for divorce here would have been pretty clear
but, unless he wanted to, there was no need for a public trial and
humiliation for Mary. Divorce could take place quietly since it
only required a written document and competent witnesses.

Angels and dreams

Throughout Old Testament tradition, people received messages
in a variety of ways, including dreams and visits by angels. These
two do not often overlap – either people saw angels or they had
a dream. There are very few occasions when angels appeared in
a dream: one is in Genesis 31.11, the others are in Matthew's
Gospel, here in the birth narrative and in the visit of the magi. It is
unclear why Matthew joined these two strands – the suggestion
that the only other occurrence of such a phenomenon includes
another Joseph (Genesis 31.11) seems far-fetched but there is
little else to explain it.

He will save his people from their sins

Unlike Luke, who makes very little of the meaning of John's
name (see pp. 85), Matthew makes much of the meaning of the
name Jesus. In the Old Testament, names given by God always
have significance – see for example Genesis 16.1; Isaiah 8.3
or Hosea 1.4. Here the Greek word *Iēsous* comes from the
Hebrew *Yeshua*, which is connected to the verb 'to save' or the
noun 'salvation'. Jesus' name then is seen by Matthew as being
an indication of what he was sent to do.

Immanuel

Jesus is actually named twice in Matthew's account, or at least
given one name (Jesus) and associated with another (Immanuel).

The English translators of the Hebrew text have made a slightly unusual decision in their translation of Isaiah 7.14. As a rule, when significant Hebrew words occur they are translated, just as all the other Hebrew words are. This is why you will not come across the words *Hosanna* or *Hallelujah* in your English Old Testaments since these are Hebrew words and are instead translated ('Save us' in the case of *Hosanna* and 'Praise the Lord' in the case of *Hallelujah*). By rights, then, Isaiah 7.14 ought to read 'She will call his name God with us', but since it is a name being referred to the Hebrew, *Immanuel* (*immanu*, 'with us' and *el*, 'God') is used. When Matthew cited the verse in Greek he kept the Hebrew word *Immanuel* in his Greek text, which implied that it was being used as a name there.

No one thinks for a moment that Jesus was actually to be called Immanuel, but there can be no doubt that the name describes him, and what he came to do and be, perfectly.

While to our ears, that Jesus was to save people from their sins is expected and normal, from a first-century Jewish perspective it is a little surprising. The salvation for which people waited was salvation from the empire – in this instance Rome – that occupied the land and oppressed God's people. The hope for redemption that was widespread at the time was focused on God's intervention to save his people from oppression and to usher in a new reign of peace, justice and righteousness. Salvation from sin was not something for which most people were looking. Indeed the suggestion that anyone other than God, outside of the temple, could forgive sins would have been a little shocking since forgiveness was tied up with temple worship and sacrifice. This passing comment sets us up to read Matthew's Gospel through a new lens – a lens that identifies the enemy of God's people not as an oppressive foreign ruler but as the power of sin that enslaves them.

Matthew and Isaiah 7.14

Matthew's use of Isaiah 7.14 is the first of a long string of quotations from or allusions to the Old Testament that Matthew uses to point to the fact that Jesus was the fulfilment of much of Old Testament expectation. It is worth reminding ourselves here that this is a similar theme to the fulfilment of expectation that occurs in Luke, differently expressed. In Luke the theme of fulfilment is introduced by wrapping a prophecy and a fulfilment of that prophecy around the prophecy of Jesus' birth. Here the theme is introduced by the inclusion of a string of Old Testament texts that Jesus can be seen to fulfil.

Arguments about the virginal conception of Jesus can often feel a little like the question of what came first, the chicken or the egg. Some argue that the only reason Mary needed to be seen as a virgin was because the unnamed young woman in Isaiah was, and the story wouldn't have fitted with this text if she weren't. Of course the opposite might equally be the case: that Mary was a young girl and a virgin and because she was a virgin the Greek translation of Isaiah 7.14 came into Matthew's mind (or the mind of those passing on the story of Jesus' birth).

It must be said that while you could argue that Matthew made Mary a virgin to fit with Isaiah 7.14, this would not really work for the Lukan tradition, which stresses Mary's virginity even more strongly than Matthew does. This suggests that the tradition of Mary's virginity has stronger roots than simply, as some argue, Matthew's attempt to make Jesus' birth fit with an Old Testament text.

On 'almah and parthenos

Another point often made is that the word 'almah means simply 'a young woman'. So, the argument goes, Matthew did not need to make Mary a virgin for the prophecy to be fulfilled in Mary.

On one level this is indeed true. 'almah does mean 'a young woman' – it is not this word but the Hebrew word betula that has the stronger resonance of 'virgin'. Betula is not used in Isaiah 7.14. What happened, however, was that the Septuagint translation legitimately translated the Hebrew 'almah as parthenos.

Parthenos, like *'almah*, has the general meaning of 'young woman' but also has the additional resonance of 'virgin'. Matthew's quotation here is close to the Septuagint's translation and probably indicates that he was using the LXX at this point (this is not always the case: sometimes he appears to translate directly from the Hebrew into his own Greek).

The arguments we have looked at so far simply skirt around the issue of whether Isaiah 7.14 can fairly be used as a prophecy of Jesus' birth or not. It is now time to address them head on. The key to understanding the issues is to read the whole passage and not just 7.14 as we normally do.

Isaiah 7.1–16 In the days of Ahaz son of Jotham son of Uzziah, king of Judah, King Rezin of Aram and King Pekah son of Remaliah of Israel went up to attack Jerusalem, but could not mount an attack against it. [2]When the house of David heard that Aram had allied itself with Ephraim, the heart of Ahaz and the heart of his people shook as the trees of the forest shake before the wind. [3]Then the Lord said to Isaiah, Go out to meet Ahaz, you and your son Shear-jashub, at the end of the conduit of the upper pool on the highway to the Fuller's Field, [4]and say to him, Take heed, be quiet, do not fear, and do not let your heart be faint because of these two smouldering stumps of firebrands, because of the fierce anger of Rezin and Aram and the son of Remaliah. [5]Because Aram – with Ephraim and the son of Remaliah – has plotted evil against you, saying, [6]Let us go up against Judah and cut off Jerusalem and conquer it for ourselves and make the son of Tabeel king in it; [7]therefore thus says the Lord God: It shall not stand, and it shall not come to pass. [8]For the head of Aram is Damascus, and the head of Damascus is Rezin. (Within sixty-five years Ephraim will be shattered, no longer a people.) [9]The head of Ephraim is Samaria, and the head of Samaria is the son of Remaliah. If you do not stand firm in faith, you shall not stand at all.

> [10]Again the Lord spoke to Ahaz, saying, [11]Ask a sign of the Lord your God; let it be deep as Sheol or high as heaven. [12]But Ahaz said, I will not ask, and I will not put the Lord to the test. [13]Then Isaiah said: 'Hear then, O house of David! Is it too little for you to weary mortals, that you weary my God also? [14]Therefore the Lord himself will give you a sign. Look, the young woman is with child and shall bear a son, and shall name him Immanuel. [15]He shall eat curds and honey by the time he knows how to refuse the evil and choose the good. [16]For before the child knows how to refuse the evil and choose the good, the land before whose two kings you are in dread will be deserted.'

The problem is that the context of the Isaiah 7 prophecy is pretty clear. The setting is around 732 BC, when the kingdoms of Syria – called Aram in Isaiah 7.1 – and the Northern Kingdom of Israel joined together in rebellion against the empire of Assyria and attempted to persuade Judah to join them. Ahaz, the then King of Judah, was petrified, and Isaiah was sent by God to reassure him that God was on his side (7.4) and would not allow the Kings of Syria and Israel to depose him in favour of their candidate the son of Tabeel (7.4–7).

God's message to Ahaz was that he should stand firm and trust in God. The sign God gave Ahaz as proof of his promise of protection was that a woman would conceive and bear a son (7.14), and by the time he knew the difference between good and evil (7.15–16) the land of the kings Ahaz currently feared would be deserted (7.16). We know from 2 Kings 16.7 that Ahaz ignored this instruction from God and sent messengers to Assyria asking the Emperor Tiglath-pileser for help.

> **2 Kings 16.7** Ahaz sent messengers to King Tiglath-pileser of Assyria, saying, 'I am your servant and your son. Come up, and rescue me from the hand of the king of Aram and from the hand of the king of Israel, who are attacking me.'

The end of the story is that Assyria swept down from the North and destroyed both Syria and the Northern Kingdom of Israel. What scholars have never been able to be certain about is who the young woman and her child were. It is possible that she was Ahaz's wife but it may also have been just someone from his court.

This throws up for us an important question: where it is clear that there was a definite historical context behind an Old Testament prophecy, is it legitimate to see it as fulfilled in an entirely different time frame? In my view the answer to this is 'yes', but only if we understand history in the terms laid out in the Introduction (see pp. iv–vi above). If the history of salvation is marked by God's dramatic intervention time and again in similar terms but different contexts, then it is not hard to see Isaiah's prophecy fulfilled both at the time of Ahaz and again at the time of Jesus. In its original context the prophecy was to a man gripped by fear about what the future would hold. The same is true of Joseph. In both contexts reassurance was needed of God's intervention in the world to save his people. If anything, the prophecy is even more fully fulfilled with the birth of Jesus than with the birth of the child to an unnamed young woman of Ahaz's day.

It is certainly not hard to see why Matthew, in particular, saw it fulfilled in glorious multicolour with the birth of Jesus to Mary, a true example of God with us.

* * *

Reflection

The question of the fulfilment of prophecy and whether Matthew was or wasn't right to see certain prophecies fulfilled in Jesus may seem to be esoteric and irrelevant but is, in fact, a vitally important question for our engagement with Scripture today. Indeed this is the very issue that has caused a lot of controversy in the writings of historical critical scholars. Historical critical scholarship, as its name suggests, is concerned to locate the Bible in its original historical context and to understand it from within that context. Whether that context be the time when the events originally took place or when they were written down, the primary focus of this kind of interpretation is to limit the meaning of the text to its location in history.

The value of this is that it has helped us understand much more about the texts and their original context; the problem is that it makes the Bible much harder to apply into our own context – or even into the context of the New Testament. It challenges us to ask whether Matthew was right or wrong to use the Old Testament as he did. Matthew most certainly stripped texts out of their original contexts (both historical and literary), something trained biblical scholars urge people not to do.

In truth this is one of the factors that has forced a gap between scholars and people of faith, and persuaded some at least that scholarship has little to offer to faithful readings of Scripture. How you respond to the conundrum is up to you but it might be helpful if I tell you how I respond to it.

As with many things, it is important to recognize that the answer to the problem does not have to be an either/or but a both/and answer. If you make it either/or, as some do, then you risk on the one hand making the Bible solely a document of historical interest but no more, or on the other hand turning it into text written solely for your own benefit and with guidance for you on every page. Of course neither of these is adequate. The Bible is neither a text that spoke only into its original context, nor one that only speaks into ours. It spoke then and continues to speak now. Understanding its historical context can help us understand more about what it is saying but doesn't restrict its message in any way.

People sometimes use the image of a bouncing bomb to describe the effect of prophecies – though I must admit to being unsure about this kind of imagery! Prophecies can be true on more than one occasion, until they reach a moment – as with Jesus' birth – when their truth comes to absolute fulfilment. It is this balance, tension even, between something being true at a particular moment and also true at other moments that makes the Bible speak so powerfully generation after generation.

Meditation

Immanuel, God with us
  Throughout our lives
  Through joys and sorrows; life and loss;
Never failing, always loving, God with us.

Immanuel, God with Ahaz
  When he needed him most
  In his terror and despite his refusal
Never failing, always loving, God with Ahaz

Immanuel, God with Mary
  In her youth
  In her courage beautifully steadfast
Never failing, always loving, God with Mary

Immanuel, God with Joseph
  At time of testing
  In his righteousness, lovingly expressed
Never failing, always loving, God with Joseph

Immanuel, God with us
  Throughout our lives,
  In youth and old age,
  When we need him most
  At times of testing
Never failing, always loving, God with us

PART 3

Arrivals

In Luke's Gospel in particular Jesus' birth is a long time coming. We wait through 56 verses for John to be born and then another 24 for the arrival of Jesus himself. By the time Jesus has been born, however, we are ready and prepared to see his birth as the start of a new era in the world, to recognize the dynamic of God's action coupled with a human response of praise, to be familiar with angels and their messages and many other themes beside, so that the story of the birth itself can be told simply, cleanly and with very little detail.

Matthew's account is even simpler and passes over the moment of Jesus' birth with barely a pause for breath, since he recognizes that important as Jesus' birth was, what came after it was even more significant.

5

The Birth of John

Luke's long first section, which comprises a total of 80 verses, comes to an end with the fulfilment of the opening promise. As we noticed above, this fulfilment is far more important than 'just' a fulfilment of God's promise to Zechariah through Gabriel. The significance of John's birth just as Gabriel predicted sets the scene for the whole story that can be found in the pages of Luke–Acts. If God is the God who keeps his promises (just as Mary has declared in the Magnificat), then God is the God who always keeps his promises. If this promise, given in verse 13, can be so clearly fulfilled in verse 57, then how much more will Jesus fulfil all that God has promised to his people? Luke sets our gaze from the start on the theme of fulfilment, a theme that will return again and again as the story unfolds.

> **Luke 1.57–63** Now the time came for Elizabeth to give birth, and she bore a son. [58]Her neighbours and relatives heard that the Lord had shown his great mercy to her, and they rejoiced with her.
>
> [59]On the eighth day they came to circumcise the child, and they were going to name him Zechariah after his father. [60]But his mother said, 'No; he is to be called John.' [61]They said to her, 'None of your relatives has this name.' [62]Then they began motioning to his father to find out what name he wanted to give him. [63]He asked for a writing tablet and wrote, 'His name is John.' And all of them were amazed.

Luke reminds us in verse 58 that Mary's song, the Magnificat, was as much a prophecy as a declaration of her own praise. In other words if God is the God who shows mercy from generation to generation then we should be on the lookout for occasions when this is demonstrated to be true. We do not have long to wait. Only three verses after the end of Mary's song we find the first example of God's mercy. The birth of a child to Elizabeth led to her neighbours' rejoicing with her. In her case God's mercy to her led to her immediate inclusion into the heart of her community. One of the impacts of a couple's inability to bear a child would have been a lurking suspicion that it was a sign to the world of God's disfavour. The consequences of this would have been a considerable level of loneliness and grief. The reversal of this led to Elizabeth's immediate re-inclusion into the heart of her community.

* * *

Reflection

One of the challenges of reading and engaging with stories about childbirth in the Bible is that the narratives appear to demand that we adopt the same attitude as they do. For some within our own culture, immeasurable grief and heartache still surrounds the question of fertility. Those who wish to have children and cannot often express a sense of loss and loneliness – a grief for someone who might have been.

It is hard then for us to begin to imagine what it might have been like to have lived in a culture in which being unable to give birth was seen as a curse and something to despise, rather than a private grief as it is today. From time to time the Bible gives us a glimpse of the pain experienced by those unable to have children: for example Rachel, who struggled to conceive, said to Jacob her husband, 'Give me children, or I shall die!' (Genesis 30.1) and Hannah's grief at her inability to bear children was so great that Eli thought she was drunk (1 Samuel 1.13).

This pain can only have been exacerbated by the cultural attitudes of the day towards those without children. Even the English word used to describe a woman who could not bear children suggests a sweeping condemnation – 'barren' is often used of soil and means sterile and of too poor a quality to be able to bear fruit. The Hebrew equivalent, 'akar, has a sense of uprootedness about it, with the implication of being torn away from the family stock and left to wither.

The problem with using such words in modern English is that the statement that someone 'was barren' seems to make an entire judgement about them: they are entirely fruitless and without purpose in the world. One of the great challenges is to read these narratives in a way that resists this global judgement while still recognizing the intense pain experienced by women like Elizabeth who had found it hard to conceive.

* * *

The tussle between Elizabeth and her neighbours over the naming of John reveals the needed response to God's mercy. God who is overwhelmingly generous and gracious nevertheless requires a response of faithfulness. Elizabeth – and Zechariah when he can speak again – demonstrate exemplary faithfulness by insisting on the naming of John as Gabriel had instructed. It is somewhat intriguing that Luke makes nothing of the meaning of the name John. In Hebrew *Yohanan*, John, means 'God has shown favour'. Given this narrative, which is all about God showing favour, it would seem to be a perfect explanation for why his name should be John. Then, again, Luke is clear that he should be called John not because of its meaning but because God decreed that it should be so. The fact that it also fits Elizabeth's circumstances may be beside the point.

Naming and circumcision

Luke conflates here the acts of circumcision and of naming. There is no evidence within Judaism of the practice of naming a

---

child at circumcision until the eighth century AD. In the first cen
tury the custom appears to be to name the child at birth.

There is no real problem here since it is simply the neighbours
who assume that the child will be called Zechariah. He could well
have been named John at birth, and this was the first occasion
on which the neighbours became aware of this and protested.
In fact in verse 63 Zechariah wrote on a small wooden writing
tablet literally 'John is his name'. This implies that his name had
already been given at birth – in fact in this instance before birth.

One of the lovely conundrums of this story is the fact that
Elizabeth knew the baby's name was to be John even though
Zechariah had been unable to speak ever since he heard the news
of this. We could explain this in a variety of ways – and it is up to
you to decide how you explain it. It may be that this reveals that
these details come entirely from Luke and that he overlooked a key
detail in laying out the story. Another option is that Elizabeth too
was visited by an angel – as indeed Matthew records that Joseph
was – and that she received the information that way.

An intriguing detail of the narrative here is that although all we are
told is that Zechariah was unable to speak, the crowd signal to him
to ask his view of the name. This implies that they assume, accurately
or not, that Zechariah can neither hear nor speak. Luke does not correct this assumption and it reveals the close association in the ancient
mind between hearing and speaking – the reality was that those who
could not hear found it very difficult to communicate with those
around them. Whether this was true of Zechariah is hard to say, but
if he had not been able to hear – or was thought unable to hear – it
would explain the crowd's astonishment when he declared the same
name that Elizabeth had.

The Benedictus

This story ends appropriately with another song, this time from
Zechariah. As with Mary's song, Luke is pointing us to an essential

dynamic of the response to God's action – the only appropriate way to respond to God is in worship. The very first thing Zechariah did when he could speak again was to praise God.

One of the interesting features of the Benedictus is that it begins with Jesus – who has not yet been born – and only later moves back to thinking about John and his role. In fact the song falls into two major parts: a blessing of God ('Blessed be the Lord God of Israel') and a prophetic proclamation of what John had come to be and do ('And you, child, will be called the prophet of the Most High'). As a result the song has strong resonance with declarative Psalms from the Old Testament that blend a celebration of the nature of God with a declaration of what God was about to do.

A slight difference between the Benedictus and the Magnificat is that where the Magnificat is full of biblical quotation and allusion, the Benedictus uses fewer stock Psalm phrases but does employ the structure of a declarative Psalm in a way that the Magnificat does not. These songs of praise, then, are close but not exact parallels of each other.

Luke 1.64-79 Immediately his mouth was opened and his tongue freed, and he began to speak, praising God. [65]Fear came over all their neighbours, and all these things were talked about throughout the entire hill country of Judea. [66]All who heard them pondered them and said, 'What then will this child become?' For, indeed, the hand of the Lord was with him. [67]Then his father Zechariah was filled with the Holy Spirit and spoke this prophecy:

[68]'Blessed be the Lord God of Israel, for he has looked favourably on his people and redeemed them. [69]He has raised up a mighty saviour for us in the house of his servant David, [70]as he spoke through the mouth of his holy prophets from of old, [71]that we would be saved from our enemies and from the hand of all who hate us.

[72]Thus he has shown the mercy promised to our ancestors, and has remembered his holy covenant, [73]the oath that he swore to our ancestor Abraham, to grant us [74]that we, being rescued from the hands of our enemies, might serve him without fear, [75]in holiness and righteousness before him all our days.

> [76]And you, child, will be called the prophet of the Most High; for you will go before the Lord to prepare his ways, [77]to give knowledge of salvation to his people by the forgiveness of their sins. [78]By the tender mercy of our God, the dawn from on high will break upon us, [79]to give light to those who sit in darkness and in the shadow of death, to guide our feet into the way of peace.'

As with Mary's song, it is worth noticing that Zechariah takes his praise from the personal to the corporate. This is no song of praise about what God has done for me – instead Zechariah locates it clearly as a salvific action for the whole of God's people. Like Mary, Zechariah stretched his vision of praise beyond his own needs to those around him. It is also worth noticing that Zechariah's song answers the question of the people in verse 66: 'What then will this child become?' The answer is that he will be called the prophet of the Most High and will go before the Lord.

Blessed be the God . . .

Within Judaism prayers often opened with a blessing to God, and it is a formula that can be found replicated in a number of New Testament prayers, such as 2 Corinthians 1.3 and Ephesians 1.3. Indeed the most famous of the *Berakhah* or blessings is the *Amidah* or 18 benedictions, which is the central prayer of the Jewish liturgy and is still said three times a day.

The popularity of its usage raises the question of what it means to bless God. It is not hard to see how God blesses us but it is much more difficult to work out how we can bless God in return. The answer seems to be that we do not in any way change God's state but what we do is to recognize, acknowledge and proclaim how wonderful he is. In other words when we bless God we do not change God but we do change ourselves as we recognize once more who God really is.

Indeed one of the profound elements of the Jewish benediction tradition is the intention of transforming the most mundane of

> daily actions into a religious experience of God's generosity. The
> regular blessing of God reminds us of all that God has done for us.

It is interesting to note that Luke tells us that Zechariah's song
of praise is a prophecy. This link is an intriguing one. Today we
would make a great distinction between praise and prophecy but
if you look carefully at the words of the Benedictus – not to mention the Magnificat – the connection becomes clear. Both songs
of praise focus on a recognition of God's action for what it was
and what it would mean for the world. As such both songs very
quickly became prophecy, declaring, in the best prophetic tradition, the impact of God's action on the world. Praise and prophecy, then, are very closely linked.

Worship in Luke

It is worth noting that a key theme that emerges time and time
again in Luke is the importance of praise. We are often reminded,
in the way Luke tells his story, that prayer and praise are a necessary response to God's goodness. Mary does it. Zechariah
does it. Simeon and Anna do it. The whole Gospel ends with the
disciples doing it in the temple – indeed it is worth noting that
Luke's 'Gentile' Gospel both begins and ends in the temple in
a way no other Gospel does. Worship is stitched through Luke's
account as the only real way to respond to God's acts of mercy
and compassion. God blesses us with goodness and in response
we bless him with praise.

The main focus of the Benedictus is redemption. It is a theme that
runs all the way through the song: from the opening verse, which
declares that God has visited his people and brought them redemption (1.68); through John's role as the one who will give knowledge
of salvation to the people by the forgiveness of their sins (1.77); to
the final couplet, which speaks of the new dawn that will break upon

God's people giving them light and showing them where to go. The song weaves together perfectly the present and the future. God has cared for his people and brought redemption (1.68; that is, it has already happened) but at the same time we still look forward to the dawn breaking upon us (1.78; that is, it has not yet happened). This balance of completed action with action yet to come sums up perfectly the dynamic of Christian existence in which we are called to constant vigilance with songs of praise for all that God has done coupled with certain hope that there is much more to come.

Visitation

In the King James Version the two verses 1.68 and 1.78 are connected through the use of the word 'visit'. This connection is obscured in more modern translations like the NRSV, which translates the word in verse 68 as 'has looked favourably on' and the word in verse 78 as 'will break upon'. In fact the same Greek word, *episkeptomai*, is used in both. This song begins and ends, then, with the twin ideas that God has visited his people and will visit his people[1] – the visit whenever it happens brings redemption and transforms the world.

---

* * *

Reflection

One of the features of Luke's birth narratives is the regular statement of what God has already done for his people. In 1.68 Zechariah declares that God '*has* looked favourably on his people and redeemed them'. In a similar way in Simeon's song (the Nunc

---

1 Some ancient manuscripts put both verbs in the past tense, the one in verse 78 as well as the one in verse 68. Scholars think this is unreliable and that when it happens a later scribe has decided that the same form of the verb should be used twice.

Dimittis), Simeon declares that his eyes *have* seen salvation. In the case of Zechariah, Jesus has not even been born, and in the case of Simeon he was, according to Luke, a mere eight days old.

The Protestant tradition often associates salvation with God's action – what God *has* done for us – an action that we see especially in Jesus' death on the cross. Luke's birth narratives require us to have a wider vision of salvation. Both Zechariah and Simeon recognize and proclaim God's salvation before Jesus has done anything at all. This reminds us that salvation is – to use Zechariah's word from the Benedictus – about God's visitation or presence. Both Zechariah and Simeon recognize that God's simple presence is enough to save and redeem, and that that was worth celebrating in song.

John grew up

> **Luke 1.80**   The child grew and became strong in spirit, and he was in the wilderness until the day he appeared publicly to Israel.

The final verse of chapter 1 contains a favourite motif of Luke. From time to time in his narrative, having devoted a vast amount of time to one period, Luke wants to move us on swiftly to the next part of the narrative. As a result, having spent almost 80 verses on a few months he then spends one verse on 30 years, fast-tracking John from birth to ministry in a few simple words.

30 years

How do we know, you might be wondering, that it is 30 years between John's birth and the start of his ministry? The answer is provided in Luke 3.23, in which Luke declares that Jesus was about 30 when he began his ministry. Since no other Gospel provides any other tradition, this is widely accepted as the rough age of Jesus when he began to minister – and hence therefore also of John the Baptist.

One feature worth noting is the importance of the Spirit here. The Spirit is significant in Luke, appearing at various key points in the narrative until, of course, the most important point of all at Pentecost in Acts 2. Unlike the other Gospels, Luke stresses the key role of the Spirit in shaping the events that unfold even before the moment of the coming in full at Pentecost. The Spirit is particularly important in the birth narratives: John is predicted by Gabriel to be filled with the Spirit (1.17); the Spirit is said to be the agent of Mary's conception (1.35); Elizabeth was filled with the Spirit and cried out (1.41); Zechariah was also filled by the Spirit before speaking the Benedictus (1.67); John is said to be strong in the Spirit here (1.80); Simeon was guided by the Spirit into the temple (2.25). In other words the Spirit played a vital role in shaping the events of God's salvation as they unfolded in Luke.

Having said that, here – as elsewhere in the New Testament – this verse could equally be translated 'strong in spirit', as it is in all the modern translations. This at first glance appears to have a very different meaning from being 'strong in the Spirit'. Being 'strong in spirit' implies to our modern ear being self-possessed, confident and having strength of character. There is no doubt that John was all of these but that doesn't seem to be the point Luke is making here. Being strong in spirit/the Spirit is in Luke – as in Paul – more closely intertwined than it is for us. Our spirit is that which allows us to commune with God's Spirit. The goal of the faithful is so to align their spirit with God's Spirit that the two intertwine. It is quite possible – probable even – that Luke means both here. John became so strong in 'spirit' that the Spirit guided him in all he did.

In the wilderness

Luke's passing reference to John being in the wilderness is worth a brief comment. It seems an odd thing to say – why would a child grow up in the wilderness? The comment is probably to be under stood theologically and intended to be seen alongside becoming strong in spirit/the Spirit.

The wilderness had strong resonance in the Old Testament. It was the place where the people first entered the land with Joshua. It was the place that Isaiah declared should be prepared for God's return in Isaiah. The wilderness was the place where God would do new things and by doing so would transform his people. The reference to John being in the wilderness until his public appearance – when incidentally he stayed in the wilderness – is designed to direct our attention to someone who was expecting the in-breaking of God into our world at any moment. This was someone who was not only spiritually attuned to God's presence but geographically located in the right place when he arrived too.

* * *

Reflection

Luke prepares us for the moment of Jesus' birth like no other Gospel writer does. The lengthy chapter 1 introduces a positive wealth of theological themes all of which, in their different ways, help us to read what follows with greater insight and clarity: themes of prophecy and fulfilment; of God's action and the need for human response in praise; of the imminence of God's visitation and accompanying redemption; of the importance of the Holy Spirit in shaping the events that unfold – to name but a few.

Luke is not just preparing us, however, for the birth of Jesus, he is preparing us to read the whole Gospel correctly. In a different way from John's Gospel, Luke is attempting to point to how to read the whole Gospel that follows. What John does through poetry, Luke does through story. These stories are much, much more than being chronological scene setters for Jesus' birth and start of ministry; they are theological scene setters for understanding the Gospel that follows. As such it is worth lingering over them and savouring their message – since once we have done that the rest of Luke – and even of Acts – will make more sense.

6

The Birth of Jesus

After lengthy preparations, especially in Luke, we arrive at last at Jesus' birth. Having had such a long run-in, the actual birth narrative itself feels quite short, with only minimal details. This is why nativity plays have to add in so many additional details: if they presented only what was in the text the whole play could be over in 5–10 minutes.

In a way, Matthew and Luke do not need to give us many more details than they have here since the significance of Jesus' birth has been so well set up in the previous passages. If we omit to read these passages then some of the theological themes and emphases in the birth narratives themselves can be lost. As a result it is important to read them all – including the genealogies – before we get to the birth narratives, so that we can understand more clearly what is going on. Some of the key themes are the divine and earthly ancestry of Jesus; that he has been long-awaited; that now is the right moment for his birth; that his birth has been foreseen both in the far and near past; that his birth signals the fulfilment of much of what God had intended to do.

The Birth of Jesus in Matthew's Gospel

Matthew 1.24–25 When Joseph awoke from sleep, he did as the angel of the Lord commanded him; he took her as his wife, 25but had no marital relations with her until she had borne a son; and he named him Jesus.

As we noted above, Matthew's Gospel does not really have a 'birth' narrative – verses 24–25 are the closest it gets to one. As with Luke's accounts, the stress is on Joseph's obedience to God's call and his willingness to fulfil what he had been commanded to do by God. In particular he took Mary as his wife and named the child Jesus.

At this point Matthew throws in an additional and fascinating detail: that Joseph (literally) 'did not know her until she had given birth to her firstborn son'. This returns us once again to debates about the virgin birth, which require us to stop and reflect one more time on the subject (see my initial reflections above, p. 60). It is clear that Matthew intends to communicate absolute clarity about who the biological father of Jesus was. If Joseph had no sexual relations with Mary before the birth of Jesus then there can be no doubt on this matter.

What is unclear is whether he is trying to tell us more than this – he has certainly been understood to be doing so through Christian history. You may remember, above, the discussion about the difference between the virginal conception and the virgin birth. Luke is clear that Mary was a virgin at the moment of conception but makes no comment about the virgin birth at all. Matthew, here, takes us one more step. In terms of sexual relationships, Mary remained a virgin at the birth of Jesus.

This quickly developed into the belief that she remained physically a virgin at the birth of Jesus; that is, her hymen remained intact. An image popular in the medieval church was that Jesus passed through Mary's shut womb like a ray of sun passes through glass. It also developed into the view that she remained a virgin after birth too – and had no children. In some but not all manuscripts Mary is said to have given birth to her firstborn son. It could imply that there were other children later, or it might simply be acknowledging the importance of the fact that she had had no other children before. In Luke the phrase has much more significance, as we shall see below.

Given the very tight definition of virgin birth in Christian history (that Mary remained a physical virgin during birth), I prefer to accept the virginal conception; the virgin birth is more difficult.

* * *

Reflection

Discussions about the virgin birth as classically defined within Christian history – that Mary was a virgin before, during and after Jesus' birth; that her womb remained 'closed' during the whole process; that the birth was painless and without trauma; that she went on to have no more children – are, to put it mildly, something I struggle with.

Mary is an inspiring character and one who inspires me more and more as time goes on. What is important to me, however, is that she was a woman *like* me. She faced the same challenges I do but with remarkable grace and courage. She experienced some of the things I have experienced. She worried for her child as I worry for mine. She mourned when he died as I would if mine died. Mary is someone – one of the few female characters in the New Testament – who stands as an inspiration for someone like me. Indeed I discover that I am not alone. Women who have borne children often relate to Mary in a particular way, but whatever your own experience, one of the most inspiring characteristics of Mary is that she was a person *like* us who did great things for God and the world.

The birth narratives inspire us all because they bring us to the recognition that God chose, willingly and gladly, to live our lives as we live them but by doing so to show us a different way of living them. If we begin to strip out details and say he was born like us – but not quite like us – then the power of the message is, in my view, diminished. What makes Mary such an inspiration is that she, an ordinary young girl, was able to welcome God into the world with tears and joy, with agony and peace, with dread and with courage, as women throughout the centuries have done and will continue to do. It is the very fact that she experienced one of the most primal, disturbing and joyful experiences of life that makes the birth of Jesus such a moving event. Such an experience does not diminish her in my eyes at all – in fact it elevates her.

The Birth of Jesus in Luke's Gospel

> **Luke 2.1–7** In those days a decree went out from Emperor Augustus that all the world should be registered. ²This was the first registration and was taken while Quirinius was governor of Syria. ³All went to their own towns to be registered. ⁴Joseph also went from the town of Nazareth in Galilee to Judea, to the city of David called Bethlehem, because he was descended from the house and family of David.
>
> ⁵He went to be registered with Mary, to whom he was engaged and who was expecting a child. ⁶While they were there, the time came for her to deliver her child. ⁷And she gave birth to her first-born son and wrapped him in bands of cloth, and laid him in a manger, because there was no place for them in the inn.

The census

One of the problems often raised by readers of the birth narratives is that whereas in Luke, Mary and Joseph clearly lived in Nazareth before the birth of Jesus and only travelled to Bethlehem for the birth, in Matthew they are recorded as being in Bethlehem for the birth and only later settling in Nazareth when they returned from exile in Egypt. In my view it is important not to make too much of this distinction. Both Gospel writers are agreed that Jesus was born in Bethlehem and grew up in his home town of Nazareth. The movement between the two places is clear in both: Luke tells us why Mary and Joseph went from Nazareth to Bethlehem (2.1) and Matthew tells us why they settled in

Nazareth later on (2.22). Beyond that the details are fuzzy. You could argue that we do not actually know where Joseph lived at the time of the annunciation in Matthew's Gospel. It is, though, worth acknowledging that if we did not have Luke's version we might fairly conclude that Mary and Joseph lived in Bethlehem at the time of Jesus' birth, only moving later.

The real question is whether you consider this to be a fundamental disagreement between the two Gospels or a mild difference in detail. In my mind this is more the latter – a mild difference. Both Gospels have Jesus born in Bethlehem and both have him growing up in the small Galilean town of Nazareth. What differs is the explanation of how he went from one to the other. Again, in my mind this can be easily explained by there being a fundamental tradition about Jesus' birth that was remembered widely but needed supplementing with additional details. It is the detail not the fundamental tradition that differs. Of course you may respond that the census is a fundamental tradition; in my mind it is not but I shall leave you to decide for yourself how important these questions are (see the discussion on pp. ix–xiv above about historicity and connected issues).

In Luke's Gospel the event that caused Joseph and Mary to move from Nazareth to Bethlehem is the census. Luke refers to this census with emphasis (2.1, 2, 3, 5), and this alerts us to the fact that he is making an important point here for his narrative. Notice that Luke moves from the whole world (2.1); to Syria (2.2); to Nazareth and Bethlehem (2.4). It is almost as though he is giving us a panning shot to establish the scene before narrowing in on Jesus and his birth. Beginning with the whole world also reminds us that, ultimately, this is not a story about a small village in either Galilee or Judea but is a world story – set on a world stage – that would change that world. Also important is the recognition of the challenge Jesus brought to the world leaders of his day. Matthew focuses on the challenge to Herod the Great; Luke on the challenge to the Roman Empire. Both are right. The very fact of who Jesus was and is challenges the power of earthly rulers, unsettling their authority and suggesting a different way of being. Luke's opening, then, reminds us that this apparently small tale will have enormous consequences.

Divine Augustus Caesar

Gaius Octavian was the grandnephew and adopted heir of Julius Caesar. After Caesar's assassination Octavian joined ranks with Mark Anthony and with Marcus Lepidus to defeat his uncle's killers. Their success saw the final demise of the Roman Republic and, eventually, the establishment of an Empire under an Emperor. Octavian slowly extracted himself from the triumvirate with Mark Anthony and Marcus Lepidus and began to term himself Gaius Julius Caesar, Son of a God. Later on he also dropped Gaius in favour of the Latin term Imperator (or commander) and added Augustus (or majestic) to the end of his name.

The placing of Jesus' birth in the context of Augustus is striking. Augustus adopted more and more titles during his lifetime, including Son of a God and majestic; Jesus at his birth was both Son of God and, despite his poverty, profoundly majestic. Augustus strove to maintain his world-conquering power; Jesus had willingly given his up. Augustus changed the world by force; Jesus by love. By stressing Augustus in his birth narrative, Luke is reminding us of how subversively different Jesus was. This tiny baby would end up confronting the greatest empire in the world.

Historical problems with the census

Luke's statement about the census is one of the most problematic historical issues of the whole of his account – it is hard to find a way to reconcile what he says here with what we know historically.

The Roman Empire did conduct censuses either for taxation purposes or prior to conscripting people to their army. The Jews were exempt from conscription so any census would have been for taxation not for conscription. There is no evidence anywhere that there was a pan-Roman Empire census at any time. The task would have been too great. The reference to the world, therefore, is more likely to be scene setting, as we noted above, than reporting what actually happened.

There was a census in Judea (not Galilee) in AD 6. Indeed Quirinius, governor of Syria, was expressly sent out to Judea for this census. The need for the census arose when Herod Archelaus was deposed by Augustus (see below) and Augustus wanted to know accurate figures for his head tax. Indeed this census caused an uproar, since it was against Jewish law to enact a census, and Judas of Galilee led an uprising that the historian Josephus attributed as the start of the zealot movement (though modern scholars think that it may in fact have started much later, around the time of the Jewish war).

Herod the Great and his successors

When Herod the Great died in 4 BC his land was split between three of his sons: Archelaus became King of Judea, Samaria and Idumea (though Augustus later downgraded this to ethnarch); Antipas became tetrarch of Galilee and Perea; Philip became tetrarch of Batanea (the territory on the other side of the Galilee from Herod Antipas but not including the Decapolis).

A king has power to rule over a country; an ethnarch is merely a governor and rules on behalf of someone else (in this instance Rome); a tetrarch rules only a portion of a country. So Judea was deemed a whole country and Herod Antipas and Philip shared the rest.

Herod Antipas ruled until AD 39 (hence he was the Herod who is mentioned again later in the Gospels at the time of Jesus' trial); Philip ruled to AD 34 but Herod Archelaus was so brutal a ruler that the Jews begged Rome to depose him and rule over them themselves. This Augustus did in AD 6, exiling Herod Archelaus to Gaul and appointing Quirinius to rule over Judea – and Samaria

---

and Idumea along with the rest of the Syrian province – in his
stead. His first task on appointment was to assess Judea for tax.
Quirinius governed Syria for six years, from AD 6 to AD 12.

Other features of the Roman censuses were that they were done
by household, and the main requirement was simply that you had
to be at home. Galilee was in a different region under the control
of Herod Antipas, so if Joseph had lived there, there would have
been no conceivable point in his travelling to Judea since his taxes
would have been paid in Galilee not in Judea.

Before Quirinius was governor of Syria

One suggestion sometimes made is that verse 2 should read:
'This was the first registration and was taken *before* Quirinius
was governor of Syria.' If this were the case then Luke would be
referring to a census unknown from Roman records that took
place before Quirinius was appointed. While it is just possible for the Greek to mean this, it would involve a very unusual
construction – *prōtē* normally only means 'before' when it is followed by a noun, not a genitive absolute – and only half solves
our problem as it points us to a census we otherwise know
nothing about.

So what are we to do, then, with these historical problems? One
option is to suggest that there was an earlier census of Galilee
and Judea – maybe while Herod the Great was still alive and the
country still united – for which there are no extant records. If
this is the case then Luke may have confused that one and the
much more famous one under Quirinius and combined the two.
Also if this were a census by Herod not by Rome, the conditions
of how people registered might have been different. Another

option is to suggest further confusion on the part of Luke, who was trying to work out why a Jesus who lived in Nazareth might have been born in Bethlehem, and fixed on a census as one explanation. There are other options too but these seem to be the main two. As with other issues, I shall leave it up to you to decide what you think, as well as how important a detail you consider it to be.

David and Bethlehem

The connection of Jesus with Bethlehem is important theologically since it allows the Gospel writers to make the significant connection between Jesus and David. This connection reminds us of how important place is within the Jewish mindset. As we noticed above, it was important that John the Baptist went out to the wilderness to be in the place where God's people first crossed into the Promised Land and the place where God promised he would return after the exile. Being there was as important as being ready. In the same way, going back to Bethlehem to David's roots is another new beginning, going back this time not to the roots of God's people in the land but to the roots of kingship and the rule over God's people by David. Jesus' being born in Bethlehem tells us much that therefore does not need spelling out in detail.

The beliefs about a Davidic descendant focus around the Jewish longing for a true return from exile. Although God's people were back in their land following the end of the exile in the Persian period, much was missing. You only have to read the Isaianic prophecies of God's glorious promises of return, peace, prosperity and unity to realize that the existence in the land was a poor shadow of what God's people hoped for. One of the striking lacks in the post-exilic world was a descendant of David. The kings went off into exile with the people but despite the mention of Sheshbazzar, a descendant of David, in some of the texts (such as Ezra 1.8), no Davidic line was ever re-established. This fact became the focus of future expectation, an expectation that over time also became intertwined with one of an anointed figure or Messiah (although priests and prophets were also anointed, the specific Davidic connection became important for the Messiah).

We learn much, therefore, about Jesus from the simple fact that Matthew and Luke take us back to Bethlehem to the place from which David was called to be king in the first place. It is worth noting that David was first called when he was a shepherd in the fields around Bethlehem – and this is exactly where Luke takes us in the next passage of his story. Again, through subtle detail Luke communicates a central theological point – that Jesus is indeed the new David who will emerge as King from the same place as his illustrious ancestor.

She gave birth to her firstborn son

One of the central details of nearly all nativity plays is that Mary went into labour on the way to Bethlehem and was so desperate for somewhere to stay that she and Joseph had to settle for a stable – or a cave – in the outhouses of a local inn. Enter the spoilsport New Testament scholar. Let us be clear that the traditional version is far to be preferred in terms of drama but is not really what the text suggests.

The firstborn son

We noted above in Matthew's account that Mary is said in some manuscripts to give birth to her firstborn son. This description is key to Luke's account and here it has a great significance. The importance of the firstborn son is that he is the one who will inherit the birthright from his father. All we know of Joseph from Luke is that his birthright was his membership of the house of David. Jesus as firstborn son, therefore, would inherit this in a way no one before him had ever done.

There is no timescale given for Joseph and Mary's stay in Bethlehem. The assumption that the baby was born as they arrived comes solely from the statement that there was 'no room in the inn'. This small phrase – with its translation 'inn' – has shaped almost the entirety of popular imaginations of what went on at Jesus' birth and is disputed by the majority of New Testament interpreters. There is little evidence to support the translation 'inn' here.

Inns were to be found almost exclusively on trade routes where there were no other houses in the vicinity. Indeed in Luke's telling of the parable of the Good Samaritan there is an 'inn' exactly where you might expect one to be. The Samaritan took the wounded man to an inn on the deserted road between Jerusalem and Jericho. The isolation of the route and the inherent danger of travelling on it made it an ideal place for an inn. The important thing to notice, however, is that when referring to the inn in Luke 10.34, Luke uses an entirely different word from the one used here in 2.7. There the word used is *pandocheion*; here it is *kataluma*. This word is used elsewhere in Luke, somewhat fascinatingly, at the last supper (Luke 22.11) to describe the guest room where Jesus and his disciples met to eat their last meal together.

This suggest that Luke uses the word in 2.7 not for an inn but for a guest room in a house. Indeed it is highly unlikely that a place like Bethlehem would have had an inn at all. Rules of hospitality dictated that people – even entire strangers – should be welcomed into your home and cared for. There would have been no need for an inn in a place like Bethlehem.

In Jerusalem the 'guest room' would probably have been a whole room as it appears to have been in Luke 22.11 (though it might have been a 'room' on the roof of the house). In smaller rural villages like Bethlehem it is more likely to have been a corner of the one-roomed abode where the whole of the family dwelt. In such houses what normally happened was that the family lived 'upstairs' on a kind of mezzanine level, with the animals on a lower level in the same space. What Luke probably envisioned was that Jesus was laid in the feeding trough of the lower level, as the upper level was so crammed with people.

There is little in the text to suggest that Mary and Joseph arrived with urgent need of accommodation; little to suggest the presence of an inn or innkeeper; nothing to suggest a search through multiple inns before finding a kind-hearted innkeeper who allowed them to stay in a stable. All of this is extraneous detail, added to make the story more engaging and dramatic. As far as I'm concerned that is fine, so long as we are clear that it is the result of an imaginative rereading of the story and not the story itself.

Swaddling bands

The practice of swaddling a baby is an ancient one and was widely practised until the seventeenth century. After a baby was born it was rubbed with salt and oil and wrapped in strips of cloth, a technique that both kept the baby warm and ensured that its limbs grew straight. There is a reference in Ezekiel 16.4 to Israel being unswaddled, which implies abandonment and neglect. Swaddling a baby, then, was a symbol of care and nurture.

---

* * *

Reflection

Much has been made, over the years, of there being no room for Jesus at his birth. There was even a carol based on the theme ('No room for the baby at Bethlehem's inn . . . No home on this earth for the dear Son of God . . . Will you still say to him "No Room"' by Hilda M. Jarvis). In other words there was a deliberate refusal of room to Jesus at his birth. The visual reason why people are reluctant to accept that the *kataluma* might have been a guest room not an inn is because all of our nativity plays would look different – but there is a theological reason too. If there was an inn, someone refused Jesus room;

if it was just a guest room, no one refused him room – he just didn't quite fit in.

Surely this is a profound theological statement itself and maybe even closer to the truth? So often we assume that people's lack of acceptance of Jesus, and all he came to be, is deliberate, thought through and clearly stated. The reality is that more often than not a refusal of Jesus is not thought through – he just doesn't quite fit into our lives. When we are busy, when so many other concerns press in all around us it is not so much that we make a decision about what to accept or not but that things slip by unnoticed. The lack of room for Jesus in our modern world is sometimes a deliberate refusal but, it seems to me, it is most often, now as then, that there simply isn't quite space for him.

* * *

The Visit of the Shepherds

Luke 2.8-20 In that region there were shepherds living in the fields, keeping watch over their flock by night. [9]Then an angel of the Lord stood before them, and the glory of the Lord shone around them, and they were terrified. [10]But the angel said to them, 'Do not be afraid; for see – I am bringing you good news of great joy for all the people: [11]to you is born this day in the city of David a Saviour, who is the Messiah, the Lord. [12]This will be a sign for you: you will find a child wrapped in bands of cloth and lying in a manger.' [13]And suddenly there was with the angel a multitude of the heavenly host, praising God and saying, [14]'Glory to God in the highest heaven, and on earth peace among those whom he favours!' [15]When the angels had left them and gone into heaven, the shepherds said to one another, 'Let us go now to Bethlehem and see this thing that has taken place, which the

Lord has made known to us.' ¹⁶So they went with haste and found Mary and Joseph, and the child lying in the manger. ¹⁷When they saw this, they made known what had been told them about this child; ¹⁸and all who heard it were amazed at what the shepherds told them. ¹⁹But Mary treasured all these words and pondered them in her heart. ²⁰The shepherds returned, glorifying and praising God for all they had heard and seen, as it had been told them.

Shepherds and their reputation

As we noticed above, the mention of the shepherds here recalls directly the start of David's calling to be king, when he too was out in the fields near Bethlehem keeping watch over his flocks. This time, however, the shepherds are not called to be king but to recognize and be the first to welcome the King. This fits well with Luke's pattern of action and response that we noticed in Chapter 1. Here again God has done something marvellous and the response of the shepherds to praise and glorify God fits in exactly with the now expected response of worship to God for what he has done for us.

There is disagreement among commentators about the significance of the shepherds' role in society. They were certainly regarded by the rabbis in the Talmud as disreputable and untrustworthy due to their semi-nomadic lifestyle. The problem was that the requirements of caring for flocks meant that they were unable to observe purity laws fully and also often ended up stealing – deliberately or accidentally – by letting their flocks stray on to other people's land. As a result they were regarded as sinners and were ineligible to give evidence in court.

Some commentators argue that this is a much later perception of shepherds and should not be anachronistically applied to the time of Jesus. Whether or not this later perception, which put shepherds in the same category as tax collectors and prostitutes, can be fairly applied at the time of Jesus, shepherds were outsiders. The requirements of caring for flocks and of following them to food put them outside the tight-knit communities of small villages like Bethlehem. Luke's emphasis on Jesus' care for the outsiders makes them the appropriate first visitors of Jesus. Their contrast with Augustus Caesar and Quirinius the governor of Syria mentioned at the start of the chapter is stark and brings to mind the Magnificat. Surely the shepherds are to be seen as the lowly in contrast to the enthroned Roman rulers? Luke has already primed us to know how the enthroned will end up.

Do not be afraid

The theme of fear in the presence of angels is one that has run through all the encounters we have observed so far. We are told that Zechariah was disturbed (the verb used, *tarassō,* can be used for boats tossed about on a sea); Mary was perplexed (though the verb used is close to the one for Zechariah this time – *diatarassō*); the shepherds, literally, 'feared with a great fear'. (See above, p. 45–6, for more on fear as a response to God and his angels.)

The visit of the angels

By now in Luke's Gospel we are accustomed to angels visiting – they have done so often since its start. As a result we are poised to look for unusual features. There are two that stand out here. The first is that, for the first time, the angel of the Lord is unnamed. Unlike in 1.19 and 26 we are not told that this is Gabriel. This may be because the angel is accompanied on this occasion by the heavenly host, or it may be that Luke assumes that we will by now know the name of the messenger of God. The other unusual feature is that the angel *is* accompanied by the heavenly host. The host of heaven appears rarely in the Bible, and when it does appear in the Old Testament it does so as God's heavenly army ready to fight (see for example 2 Kings 6.14–17). At other times, and much more commonly, the host of heaven is reported to be around the throne of God worshipping day and night (see 1 Kings 22.19). The appearance of the host in worship to people on earth, as here at Jesus' birth, is unique. The implication is that this event is so great and world changing that the shepherds are given a rare glimpse into heaven to see the angels praising God.

The host of heaven and stars

One of the intriguing features of mentions of the host of heaven is that the host is used interchangeably to refer to stars (for example Deuteronomy 4.9), to God's army (2 Kings 6.14–17) and to the angels around God's throne (1 Kings 22.19). Indeed in Judges 5.20 it is said that the stars fought from heaven. This odd reference may in fact give us the clue to what is going on here. If you imagine the world as the biblical writers would have imagined it, with the sky as our ceiling but the floor of God's dwelling place, then looking upwards would mean that you might catch a glimpse of heaven. The stars, then, in their multitudes could easily be understood to be the multitudes of the angels in heaven worshipping God. As a result it is not at all hard to see how the two could be intertwined in the minds of people like Luke.

What is significant is the words the angels sang at Jesus' birth: 'Glory to God in the highest heaven, and on earth peace'. These two themes – the glory of God and the peace of his people – are themes of the hope of God's intervention in the world that run through the prophets, especially Isaiah (see for example Isaiah 40.5; 60.19). When Isaiah looked forward to the return from exile, two themes intertwined: that all the world would see the glory of God and that peace would reign among his people. The angels, therefore, are singing much, much more than 'just' with joy at the birth of a child. They are announcing – as Zechariah did and as Simeon will shortly – that the long-awaited time has now come; that God has returned to his people; that salvation is in the world and that the world will never be the same again.

Peace and the Pax Romana

We have been noticing in Luke's account the importance of encountering the birth of Jesus against the backdrop of the Roman Empire. Luke's telling of the story makes it very clear that this gentle tale of the birth of a baby is one that strikes at the heart of the power of Rome. The angels' message of 'peace' reminds us of this. Pax Romana or 'the peace of Rome' was established by Augustus after his defeat of Mark Anthony. His task in doing this was to persuade the Romans – whose very identity had been shaped by war – of the prosperity that could come when they embraced peace. The Pax Romana became the feature that established the continuing success of the Empire in the years and decades that followed the crumbling of the Republic.

This peace, however, was enforced by military might and involved not just the cessation of war but the ensuring that all enemies were subjugated and no longer had the power to fight back. The infant Jesus represented an entirely different 'pax': it was established through love not might, through self-sacrifice not military prowess, and benefited the marginal and the outcasts not those who yearned to cling to power. The angels' message reminds us that this King and his kingdom were the opposite of the kingdoms of his day.

Again it is worth noting Luke's theme that the world has changed and salvation has come – before Jesus has done anything at all. At the time of the angels' song all he is doing is lying in a manger wrapped in swaddling bands. Luke reminds us that salvation is not so much about what has been done as it is about God's visitation to earth. Jesus is here and so salvation *has* come.

Glory of the Lord shone around them

The glory of God is an important strand that runs all the way through the Old Testament. Although there is a tradition that you cannot see God and live (see the comment on John 1.18 above,

p. 26), there is an equal and balancing tradition that you can: that on special occasions key people could and did encounter God. Often when they did so, what they encountered was the glory of God. God's glory, therefore, is that of God which we can encounter as opposed to that which we cannot. God's glory rested on the top of Mount Sinai at the giving of the law and filled the temple when he dwelt among his people. It indicated something of the awe and majesty of God's very being.

One of the ways the awe and majesty of God was communicated was through the idea that God's glory was shiny. So, for example, in Exodus 34, when Moses spent time with God on the top of Mount Sinai, as he came down the mountain his face shone. This tradition of God's glory shining grew in strength until in Luke 2 it is the most obvious thing for God's glory to do – the glory of the Lord shone around them. The implication of this is that it did so because for a moment or so heaven opened and the shepherds were invited to see into heaven itself. The host of heaven, coming as they did from the very presence of God, were suffused with his glory and shone with it, giving the shepherds a glimpse of what the glory of heaven was like.

Saviour, Messiah, Lord

In many ways the angelic announcement of Jesus' birth to the shepherds is very similar to the angelic announcement of John's birth to Zechariah and Jesus' birth to Mary. There is an appearance of an angel, the reaction of fear, an announcement of the birth, a naming of Jesus and a sign offered of the veracity of what had been said. The only difference is that this time the shepherds did not need to wait to find out the truth of the sign – instead they went with haste to see what had happened.

It is worth pausing over the name of Jesus that was announced to the shepherds. The angel did not announce that he would be called Jesus, or not quite. In a way this is appropriate because

Jesus still had to be named formally by his parents. What the angel did announce was that he was (literally) 'saviour, who is Christ, Lord'. You will remember that the name Jesus is derived from the Hebrew word for saviour; the word used here is the Greek word *sōtēr*, not the Hebrew *Yeshua* or its transliterated form, Jesus. Alongside this come two other hugely important words: Christ (the Greek word for the Hebrew Messiah) and Lord.

'Lord' has already been used a number of times in Luke's Gospel to talk of God. So Zechariah and Elizabeth were said to walk in all the ordinances and commandments of the Lord (1.6); the angels appearing have been said to be angels of the Lord (1.11; 2.9) and so on. In other words 'the Lord' has been used in the way we would have expected it to be used – to refer to God. On the other hand Luke has also introduced us to someone else – the Emperor Augustus – who was also regularly addressed as 'Lord'. These two uses point us to the fact that the angel's announcement of the 'name' of the child to the shepherds was significant.

The first two titles go together quite well. The Messiah, who was expected by many Jews to be a descendant of David, was looked for so that he could 'save' his people from the Romans and any other oppressors around. The addition of 'Lord' makes this an entirely different statement. Not only would the Saviour/Messiah save his people from the Romans, he would stand in direct conflict with Roman power as true Lord of the world. He was the Lord even as a baby. Over the years New Testament scholars have spent a long time discussing titles for Jesus and whether Son of God or Son of Man have within them expectations of divinity. It seems to me that the much more important title here is 'Lord', which Luke has used up to this point to talk about God. There seem little grounds to assume that he has suddenly sucked all divine meaning from the word now it has been attributed to Jesus.

Amazement and pondering

The shepherds respond to what they had been told in the way that Luke hopes all hearers of his story will respond – they made known what had been told to them (2.17) (and also glorified and praised God, which by now we know to be the correct response to God's action).

The response to the shepherds' message matches the responses we have already seen. The verb *thaumazō* ('wonder', 'marvel', 'be amazed'/'astonished') runs throughout Luke. The people did it as they waited for Zechariah outside the temple (1.21); they did it again when Zechariah declared his baby's name to be John (1.63); they do it here (2.18); Mary and Joseph did it after they met Simeon and Anna – and so on. Amazement at what God has done is the first step of response to Jesus but it requires further and greater steps. In Mark's Gospel the crowd never gets past its amazement at Jesus. In Luke this is not quite so strong a theme but it does raise for us the question of what the next step after amazement looks like.

On one level Luke has already answered this question – the proper response to God is not amazement but worship. In verse 19, however, he suggests an additional appropriate response. Mary treasured these words and pondered them. The first word, *suntēreō*, has the resonance of preserve or defend; in other words she made the conscious decision to protect them and while she did that she chewed over them. The second word, *sumballō*, is often used to describe a conversation. It isn't quite clear in this sentence where the words 'in her heart' should go – did she keep them in her heart or keep them and ponder them in her heart? It doesn't really matter. What does matter is that Mary conversed with herself about them: she did not allow the wonder of the event to come and go slipping past her in the press of life but actively preserved everything she knew about it and then discussed with herself its meaning. The model of reflection seems an important one for thinking about and responding to Jesus.

* * *

Reflection

Part of the power of Luke's birth narratives are the sparse details he provides. There is much more he doesn't tell us than he does. Where *do* Mary and Joseph stay in Bethlehem? How did the shepherds find them? How many shepherds were there – two or more than two? What was the response of the visitors in the overcrowded house to these odd nocturnal visitors? Other than Mary, did anyone else remember these events and wonder what they might mean? How did Joseph react?

It is the sparseness of Luke's account that requires us to enter the story imaginatively and to supply some of the missing characters. The problem we face today is that the supplied details have taken the status of canonical text and it is very difficult indeed to suggest alternative imaginative details.

Luke himself, however, suggests how we should respond to 'these words': we should follow the example of Mary – preserving the stories in our hearts, pondering the stories in our hearts and wondering what they might mean for us. It may be that if we do this and carry on doing it, our imaginative tellings and retellings of the story might become richer; we might imagine new characters into the tableau – characters excluded by traditional renderings of the tale. We might linger a little to feel the terror of the shepherds, the joy of the angels, the wonder of the villagers. We might sit for a while with Mary as she pondered what had happened. And as we do all of this we might recapture some of the wonder of that very first Christmas and find ourselves hurrying, like the shepherds, to share the good news that we have seen and heard.

Meditation

The birth of a baby is
  wonderful and terrifying;
  terrible and beautiful

A baby is born
  through pain and with joy;
  with love and through fear

The birth of a baby is
  precarious and marvellous;
  mysterious and gritty

A baby is born
  with screams of agony;
  and shouts of delight

At the moment of birth
  death and life greet each other

The birth of that baby was no different;
  poised between life and death, God came to us
  a tiny human form, with immense stature

PART 4

Aftermaths

Just as we needed a long preamble to prepare ourselves to understand the wonder of Jesus' birth, so too we need a few examples of what happened afterwards to reinforce in our minds quite what impact it had on the world. Luke's story of 'aftermath' is the story of the incipient recognition of the salvation that had come to the world; Matthew's account is altogether less welcoming. Alongside the account of the magi or wise men travelling to welcome Jesus are the first hints of the trouble that Jesus' presence would evoke among those who currently held power in the world into which he was born. Luke's tale of the striking of a blow at the heart of the Roman Empire is, of course, left at just that for now – the ramifications will unfold later in Jesus' life. But Matthew's tale has a much more pressing outcome as Herod the Great understands something of the impact of Jesus' birth on his power.

7

Herod and the Magi

If I were to order this book chronologically – as far as that would be possible for the birth narratives – then strictly speaking the encounter with Simeon and Anna might come before the visit of the magi. As many people know, the implication of the text is that this event could have happened as much as two years after the birth of Jesus, whereas Jesus' visit to the temple happened only a matter of weeks later. Ordering the accounts like this, however, would mean ending the book on a slaughter (which is not often deemed a good idea) and more importantly reversing the order of the events in the Christian year (Epiphany – or the feast of the magi – is celebrated in the West on 6 January and Candlemas – or the feast of the presentation in the temple – is celebrated on 2 February). In addition, it is a while since we have heard anything from Matthew, so it would be good to turn to his account here.

The Arrival of the Magi from the East

Matthew 2.1–8 In the time of King Herod, after Jesus was born in Bethlehem of Judea, wise men from the East came to Jerusalem, ²asking, 'Where is the child who has been born king of the Jews? For we observed his star at its rising, and have come to pay him homage.' ³When King Herod heard this, he was frightened, and all Jerusalem with him; ⁴and calling together all the chief priests and scribes of the people, he inquired of them where the

> Messiah was to be born. ⁵They told him, 'In Bethlehem of Judea; for so it has been written by the prophet: ⁶"And you, Bethlehem, in the land of Judah, are by no means least among the rulers of Judah; for from you shall come a ruler who is to shepherd my people Israel."' ⁷Then Herod secretly called for the wise men and learned from them the exact time when the star had appeared. ⁸Then he sent them to Bethlehem, saying, 'Go and search diligently for the child; and when you have found him, bring me word so that I may also go and pay him homage.'

The Date of Jesus' Birth

The timing of Jesus' birth, according to Matthew, is not easy to tie down – and Matthew does not help us much. The reign of King Herod stretched from around 37 BC to 4 BC. This means, as we noted above, Jesus couldn't have been born while Quirinius was governor of Syria. In addition, since Augustus was Emperor from 27 BC to AD 14 this does not narrow down our options much. One solution sometimes offered to the question of date is that of the star. In the ancient world it was believed that at the birth of each significant person a new star would appear in the heavens that would shine as brightly as that person's stature deserved, and would remain in the heavens until their death. If a previously unrecognized star had appeared close to the near conjunction of the planets Jupiter (the royal planet) and Saturn (the star of Saturday), which took place in 7/6 BC, then this might have been sufficient to indicate to the magi that Jesus had been born. Its appearance at his birth would also then give time for them to travel from their home before Herod died in 4 BC. Therefore 7/6 BC is a possible date for Jesus' birth, but suggested and possible dates range between 7 and 4 BC and the lack of evidence available means we cannot be too confident on the final dating.

Why wasn't Jesus born in the year zero?

There are two reasons. The first is that on our calendar there wasn't a year zero. Our calendar goes straight from 1 BC to AD 1, the 'zero' moment being just that – a moment not a year. According to Dionysius Exiguus, the sixth-century abbot who compiled our current calendar, Jesus was born in 1 BC but most would now accept that he miscalculated by a few years (and also wasn't aware of modern critical scholarship).

It is also worth noting that there is nothing in the text to suggest that the magi visited Jesus immediately. Indeed it is often pointed out that Herod commanded all children under the age of two to be killed, which suggests that there might have been a gap of up to two years between the birth of Jesus and the visit of the magi. Again all we have to go on is supposition. If the star appeared at the moment of Jesus' birth and if the magi set out at that point, then they arrived as long after that point as it took them to get there. Two years seems to be an excessive amount of time for travelling but one year does not. In any case, Matthew's story of a star appearing, the magi recognizing it and travelling to Bethlehem does suggest a delay, unless the star shone from the time of Jesus' conception.

Wise men from the East

Another factor in the timing is the question of where the magi were travelling from. Again Matthew offers us few helpful clues. The word *magus* when used technically referred to a member of a priestly caste from the Medes and the Persians. They were renowned for having particular skill in the interpretation of dreams. Indeed the story of Daniel 2 is set against this background, in which the king's dream interpreters were unable to interpret his dreams so Daniel did instead. By the time of Jesus, however, the word was no longer used technically to refer only to this priestly caste but was expanded to refer to astrologers and soothsayers, then also to magicians and sorcerers and finally to quacks and con artists. This is certainly how the word was used in Acts 13.6 where Paul and Barnabas meet someone called Bar-Jesus, who was a false prophet and a magus.

Chief priests and scribes

It is further interesting to notice that once the wise men arrived, Herod summoned his own 'wise men'. The fact that these are chief priests and scribes tells us that Herod believed them to be the equivalent of the magi – priests and experts in the written law.

The term 'chief priests' is a loose one. It does not imply that there was more than one high priest, instead it refers to the 'senior priests' of the temple, which included the high priest and his predecessors but also the captain of the temple and the temple overseers and treasurers.

There is nothing at all in Matthew to suggest that the magi were charlatans. Indeed they are portrayed as righteous people to Herod's unrighteousness. They do, however, appear to be astrologers and, although they have a dream themselves, do not appear to be particularly focused on the dreams of others. As a result they were probably astrologers from somewhere east of Jerusalem. This could be Persia or Arabia but Matthew does not see fit to narrow it down. There is no reason why he would. He, like the other Jews of his day, split the world into God's people and the rest. The magi fall into the category of the 'rest'; precisely where in 'the rest' they come from is not really the point.

What is the point is that, in Matthew's profoundly Jewish Gospel, the very first people able to recognize who Jesus was and who came to worship him were from 'the rest', the Gentiles, those whom Jews believed to have no religious sensibilities at all. The opening out of this good news from just God's people to the whole world – an opening out confirmed in the great commission in Matthew 28.19 – has already begun at Jesus' birth.

Bethlehem of Judea

In Luke's account of Jesus' birth the significance of Bethlehem seems to be tied largely to its being David's home town. Matthew's explanation of the importance of Bethlehem as the birthplace of Jesus takes a slightly different path. Here the importance of Bethlehem is attributed to Micah's iconic prophecy about a ruler coming from Bethlehem to shepherd God's people. Of course the two overlap because Micah's prophecy depends on the tradition about a successor for David coming to lead his people. This is even truer of the original verse in Micah, which reads:

> **Micah 5.2** But you, O Bethlehem of Ephrathah, who are one of the little clans of Judah, from you shall come forth for me one who is to rule in Israel, whose origin is from of old, from ancient days. NRSV

Clearly David, here, is deemed to be from 'ancient days' and the one from whom the new ruler is to be descended. This alerts us to the fact that Matthew's version of Micah 5.2 differs from both the Hebrew and the Greek texts. It reads (my translation):

> 'And you Bethlehem, land of Judah, you are by no means least among the leaders of Judah, for from you will come out a leader who will tend my people Israel.' (Matthew 2.6)

The Hebrew text of Micah 5.2 reads (my translation):

> 'But you Bethlehem Ephrathah, being little among the tribes of Judah, from you will come out for me one who will rule Israel and who has come forth from before, from ancient days.'

The Greek LXX text reads (again my translation):

> 'But you Bethlehem of the house of Ephrathah, you are smallest in the group of a thousand [that is, a tribe] of Judah from you will come out for me one ruling in Israel and his coming out will be from the beginning, from the ages of days.'

Some changes are relatively small and easy to explain. For example, 'Ephrathah' is a slightly technical reference that Matthew's audience might not really have understood. Replacing it with 'land of Judah' makes what is being said much clearer (there was a Bethlehem in the Galilee about six miles north of Nazareth).

Ephrathah

Micah's inclusion of Ephrathah was important even though it makes no sense to later audiences. 1 Samuel 17.12 tells us that Jesse was an Ephrathite from Bethlehem of Judah. The book of Ruth (1.2) also refers to Ephrathites from Bethlehem. The implication, then, is that Ephrathites were a family group, a sub-tribe of Judah, who had settled in the region of Bethlehem so that the two names had become overlapping.

Other changes are more complex. The first of these is that Matthew's version completely changes the status of Bethlehem from being 'little' (Hebrew) or 'least' (Greek) to being 'by no means least'. Micah's version reflects an accurate view of Bethlehem. The tribe of Judah settled in the least affluent part of the land – much of it is desert – and Bethlehem was one of the smallest and most insignificant towns of Judah. Micah's point is that Bethlehem was the lowest of the low but from its people God had brought the greatest of all great leaders. Over the years Bethlehem's status had not changed but still Bethlehem could produce a great leader. Matthew's adaptation of Micah's text appears to indicate that he disagreed and that, since David came from

Bethlehem, it could no longer be deemed to be the least of all towns.

The other difference is that Matthew has inserted 'who will tend my people Israel' into the text after 'a leader'. The phrase is taken from 2 Samuel 5.2 and the dedication of loyalty made by the tribes of the south (including Judah) to David at Hebron:

---

2 Samuel 5.1-2 Then all the tribes of Israel came to David at Hebron, and said, 'Look, we are your bone and flesh. [2]For some time, while Saul was king over us, it was you who led out Israel and brought it in. The Lord said to you: It is *you who shall be shepherd of my people Israel*, you who shall be ruler over Israel.'

It is clear that the connection has been made with this passage in Matthew's mind by the reference to David and the use of the word 'ruler'. The interesting question – to which we cannot know the answer – is whether he was aware that he had changed the wording of the passage or whether what we have here is the wording as he remembered it, and so intertwined were these passages in his mind that he elided them.

Herod the Great

It is worth pausing with Herod the Great for a while in order to understand some of the nuances of Matthew's narrative here. One of the characteristics of Herod that comes over strongly in this passage and the next – the slaughter of the innocents – is Herod's obsessive, paranoid defence of his kingship. This is something that is known about from a number of contemporaneous records so that although there is no historical record of Herod's slaughter of the babies in Bethlehem, scholars of Herod are agreed that he could easily have done something like that.

Herod's father was from Edom (called Idumea in Latin). The Edomites were regarded by some of the prophets as enemies of Judah because they plundered the land after Judah was taken into exile. Herod's mother was Nabatean (an ancient Arab people), the daughter of an influential nobleman from Petra. The first point about Herod to notice, therefore, is that although he was a practising Jew, his ancestry was Arab. Those Judeans whose concern was purity of line would have despised Herod's roots and considered him insufficiently Jewish. Also important was that he had no claim whatsoever to the throne. After the exile, as we noted above, the Davidic kings did not return to the throne. When there were kings again they came from the line of the Maccabees, who had led the rebellion against the Greek Seleucid empire in the second century BC and driven them out of the land. One of Herod's problems was that as he was from neither a Davidic nor a Maccabean line (in fact he was from an altogether hated line of Edomites and Nabateans), to say he had no real right to be king was to put it mildly.

Herod was king solely because of his relationship with the Romans. His father welcomed Pompey when he invaded Palestine in 63 BC and began a long period of favour from the Romans. This culminated in 37 BC with Augustus making Herod king. He embarked on massive building projects in Caesarea, Sebaste and Herodium and also completely rebuilt the temple in Jerusalem.

Despite outward success there is much evidence of Herod's inner torment. He had married Mariamne, a descendant of the Maccabees, in the hope of shoring up popularity, and he did, according to accounts, love her. Nevertheless he ended up murdering her, her two sons, her brother, her grandfather and her mother, all because he feared that they would usurp his power. Later on he also disinherited and killed his firstborn son Antipater. All this seems to have been fuelled by his knowledge that his power was based on shaky foundations and could easily be challenged by anyone who had more right to rule than he. When gripped by the fear of such a person he would murder them, even if that person was his own wife.

It is not hard to imagine, therefore, Herod's terror at the announcement by the magi that a real King of the Jews had been born, and born from the line of David in the city of Bethlehem. Such news would almost certainly have sent him into a defensive frenzy.

Reflection

Matthew's account, even more than Luke's, stresses the precarious and risky nature of Jesus' birth as a baby. The story of the incarnation is a story of risk inspired by love. So great was God's love for us that he was prepared to risk everything to come to earth as a baby. Not only were there the usual risks of infant mortality but additional risks to Jesus' infant life caused by being who he was. He was born into a world in which people, particularly Herod in this instance, were prepared to do anything to hang on to the power they had.

The story, as Matthew tells it, brings to mind Philippians 2.6 and the great gulf that exists between Jesus and Herod. Herod had very little right at all to have the position he had and so clung on to it with every fibre of his being, prepared even to kill his wife if necessary. Jesus, though he was in the form of God, did not consider this a thing to cling to but emptied himself, taking the form of a slave. Herod stands as a powerful anti-type to Christ in this story and reminds us of the importance of 'having the mind of Christ'.

Power is a slippery, destructive force. It seduces us into thinking we need to grasp at it and having grasped at it to hold it as tight as we can, lest anyone else wrest it from our grasp. The more we care about power, the tighter we hold on to it; and the tighter we hold on to it, the harder we will fight anyone else who appears to us to challenge us. The way of Christ demands that we let power go, completely, utterly and with serenity. It calls us to follow him in risking everything for the sake of love. Herod stands as a terrifying parable of what happens to people who cannot do this.

* * *

The Worship of the Magi

> **Matthew 2.9–12** When they had heard the king, they set out; and there, ahead of them, went the star that they had seen at its rising, until it stopped over the place where the child was. [10]When they saw that the star had stopped, they were overwhelmed with joy. [11]On entering the house, they saw the child with Mary his mother; and they knelt down and paid him homage. Then, opening their treasure-chests, they offered him gifts of gold, frankincense, and myrrh. [12]And having been warned in a dream not to return to Herod, they left for their own country by another road.

Nations shall come to your light

One of the passages Matthew may have in mind in the telling of his story of the magi's visit to Jesus is Isaiah 60.3 and 6. In this passage Isaiah presents a vision of God's glorious future, when God's people would return from exile, peace and prosperity would reign and the golden age of David would return. Part of this glorious future would involve the nations of the earth coming to Israel, as they had done when the Davidic line was on the throne (see the visit of the Queen of Sheba in 1 Kings 10.1–10), bringing with them precious gifts like gold and frankincense.

> **Isaiah 60.3, 6** Nations shall come to your light, and kings to the brightness of your dawn. [6]A multitude of camels shall cover you, the young camels of Midian and Ephah; all those from Sheba shall come. They shall bring gold and frankincense, and shall proclaim the praise of the Lord.

This tradition did not stop with Isaiah. Later non-biblical texts, such as the Psalms of Solomon 17.31 and 1 Enoch 53.1, also look forward to a time when nations would come from the ends of the earth with gifts to present to the chosen one.

The visit of the magi, then, functions a little like the angelic pronouncement in Luke's Gospel that the moment God's people had been waiting for had arrived (see pp. 109–10 above). Here Isaiah's prophecy was coming true. People from the nations were coming to the light and the brightness of God's new dawn, bringing with them gold and frankincense. Isaiah's promised moment had arrived and, as in Luke's Gospel, the world was now transformed.

The guiding star

In verse 9 the star appears to change from being the kind of star observed by astrologers into something much harder for us, as a modern audience, to get our heads around. Now it appears to be a guiding star going ahead of the magi to Bethlehem. One of the interesting points to notice is that, according to Matthew, the magi no longer needed the star. Herod's own wise men had told them where to look for Jesus – and that was where he was. Bethlehem was not a large town in those days and it would not have been hard to locate the child they sought.

The text begins to make sense, however, when we remind ourselves of the overlap in Jewish thinking between angels and stars (see pp. 108–9 above). The Old Testament tradition has a strand of God going before people to guide them in the way (see for the example the pillar of cloud and of fire in Exodus 13.21). Although angels are not as important in Matthew as in Luke, they do appear at crucial moments to guide people. The most obvious explanation, then, of the guiding star is that it was an angel going before them to show them the way.

The house

Some people make much of the fact that the magi enter a house here in the story (not a stable or a cave), and argue that this must

---

mean that Mary and Joseph have now moved to different accommodation. As we noted above, however (pp. 103–4), the reference to the *kataluma* and the feeding trough could well be a reference to a house. As a result there is less to be made of this reference to a house than might at first be believed.

Gold, frankincense and myrrh

The Early Church Fathers associated the three gifts with the elements of who Jesus was: gold for a king; frankincense for God; myrrh for a burial (see for example Irenaeus, *Adversus Haereses* 3.9.2). The problem with this is myrrh. Myrrh was used as a burial spice but not only as that. It was also used as a perfume, as an ingredient in incense, as a holy anointing oil and as an analgesic. Indeed its use as a perfume alongside frankincense is stressed three times in the Song of Solomon (3.6; 4.6, 14).

The association with burial might have been able to be defended had Matthew not got a different version of what was offered to Jesus on the cross: in Mark it was wine mixed with myrrh (15.23); in Matthew it was wine mixed with gall (that is, something bitter, 27.34). As a result Matthew himself does not pick up this strand in his later text.

It seems more likely, then, that the references to gold, frankincense and myrrh are allusions to the rich gifts (including perfume) that were brought to the kings of old (like Solomon) and that this is a fulfilment of that strand of expectation that said that once God returned to his people, these visits with gifts would begin again.

How many?

It is an obvious point but nevertheless worth making that we simply do not know how many magi there were. The Greek word is plural so could refer to any number from two upwards. The names of the gifts do not help us as there is no implication that one brought gold, another frankincense and another myrrh.

They paid him homage

You can always tell when a word is hard to translate because the English translations do not agree over the word to use. This is one of those occasions.

In 2.11 the NRSV says that the magi 'paid homage' but the ESV and the NIV that they 'worshipped him'. There is, of course, a vast difference between simply paying homage to someone you believe to be a king and worshipping someone you believe to be divine. Unfortunately the Greek word, *proskuneō*, is not much help here since it describes posture but not intent. The verb refers to the practice of prostrating oneself before a king or something holy, and can legitimately mean either – and the problem is that Matthew appears to use the word with both meanings.

So it is used in Matthew 4.9 when the devil invited Jesus to fall down and 'worship him'; it is also used in 8.2 when a leper came and 'knelt' before him; it is used again when the Canaanite woman begged Jesus to help her daughter (15.25); and yet again after Jesus' resurrection when disciples met him on the mountain (28.17). This is one of those words whose meaning shifts according to context. The challenge here is to work out what we think the magi were doing – paying homage or worshipping. It may be that Matthew is deliberately vague here in order to evoke that question in our minds.

Warned in a dream

The early part of Matthew contains many dreams. In 1.20; 2.13; 2.19 Joseph receives a message in a dream from an angel. Here, 2.12, and in 2.22, first the magi (2.12) and then Joseph (2.22)

have a dream without an angel (another dream, this time to
Pilate's wife with a message but without an angel, also occurs
in Matthew 27.19). Matthew does not seem to make much of
a distinction between the two. For him dreams appear to be as
effective a way of communicating as by direct angelic messenger.

* * *

Reflection

A question that often occupies me is what happened to the characters we meet in the Gospels after we meet them. In John what
happened to Nicodemus or the Samaritan woman? In the Synop-
tics what became of Simon of Cyrene or the Gerasene demoniac?
Did that single encounter with Jesus change everything for ever
or just for a few days, weeks or months? Here that question rings
out loud and clear. What happened to the magi? Indeed how you
read what they did when they finally found Jesus – did they pay
homage or worship him? – begins to answer this question. How
important an encounter was it? Did it change their lives for ever
or just for that short trip? It is a question T. S. Eliot played with
in his poem 'Journey of the Magi' as he portrayed them return-
ing home no longer at ease with how things were.

The more I think about it, however, the more I wonder
whether this is, in fact, the wrong question. It is a natural part
of human nature to assume that if something is right it is right
for ever. If you stop something and declare it to be no longer
helpful, then the assumption often made is that it never was
helpful. It was always wrong. Indeed there are many traditions
in many churches that seem to me to be kept going simply to
avoid the implication that they were never right.

The Gospel writers seem to counsel us against this. Perhaps
this is why they so rarely tell us what happened later. An
encounter with Jesus Christ, Son of God, is precisely that – an

encounter with him. Whether the effects of that encounter lasted or faded away – like the seed in the parable of the Sower – is not relevant for the encounter itself. The magi could have worshipped Jesus deeply, profoundly and genuinely, even if later the effects of that encounter faded. It might have faded in some but not all of them. It might even have gone underground to re-emerge later. The point seems to be that we should evaluate each moment for the moment it is. Whether that moment grows and bears fruit or not is a relevant question for later, but does not affect the genuineness of the encounter when it happened.

* * *

The Flight to Egypt

Matthew 2.13-23 Now after they had left, an angel of the Lord appeared to Joseph in a dream and said, 'Get up, take the child and his mother, and flee to Egypt, and remain there until I tell you; for Herod is about to search for the child, to destroy him.' [14]Then Joseph got up, took the child and his mother by night, and went to Egypt, [15]and remained there until the death of Herod. This was to fulfil what had been spoken by the Lord through the prophet, 'Out of Egypt I have called my son.'

[16]When Herod saw that he had been tricked by the wise men, he was infuriated, and he sent and killed all the children in and around Bethlehem who were two years old or under, according to the time that he had learned from the wise men. [17]Then was fulfilled what had been spoken through the prophet Jeremiah: [18]'A voice was heard in Ramah, wailing and loud lamentation, Rachel weeping for her children; she refused to be consoled, because they are no more.'

[19]When Herod died, an angel of the Lord suddenly appeared in a dream to Joseph in Egypt and said, [20]'Get up, take the child and

his mother, and go to the land of Israel, for those who were seeking the child's life are dead.'
²¹Then Joseph got up, took the child and his mother, and went to the land of Israel. ²²But when he heard that Archelaus was ruling over Judea in place of his father Herod, he was afraid to go there. And after being warned in a dream, he went away to the district of Galilee. ²³There he made his home in a town called Nazareth, so that what had been spoken through the prophets might be fulfilled, 'He will be called a Nazorean.'

One of the great differences between Luke's angelic messengers and Matthew's dream accounts is that Luke's messengers announce a future event, describe what will/should happen and then return whence they came; the dreams in Matthew actually affect the events as they happen. In Matthew, as a result of a dream Joseph decided not to divorce Mary, the magi decided to take a different route home and, here, Joseph fled with Mary and Jesus to Egypt. Luke's messages therefore are more grandly prophetic and declaratory; Matthew's messages affect the details of existence – and save Jesus' life.

It is a slight but interesting difference. The messages Luke's messengers bring are much more about giving meaning and pointing to fulfilment; the ones Matthew's messengers deliver are more about changing what was about to happen so that God's will could be done.

Fleeing to Egypt

Egypt was a common place to flee to in Old Testament literature. A couple of examples of this include Jeroboam who fled there when Solomon sought to kill him (1 Kings 11.40) and the people left at the exile who fled there after Gedaliah was assassinated (2 Kings 25.26). As Judah's near neighbour but with a very different type of ruler, it was the ideal place to seek refuge in a time of crisis.

Matthew is aware of the irony of this, however, hence the quotation from Hosea 11.1, which reads: 'When Israel was a child, I loved him, and out of Egypt I called my son.' The place from which God's people needed freeing at the time of the Exodus was the very place that was now offering refuge to God's own Son. At the same time the occasion of the Exodus was what brought about the possibility of redemption and new life in the Promised Land. Just as John was to go out to the place where the people first crossed into the Promised Land, so Jesus went to the place in which the whole story began – Egypt.

The slaughter of the children

As we observed above, Herod's character was such that it is entirely believable that he might have engaged in the kind of indiscriminate slaughter described here. Nevertheless this account only occurs in Matthew's Gospel, and you might expect such an act of brutality to have been recorded somewhere.

It is worth reminding ourselves, however, that at the time of Jesus, although the population of Bethlehem was larger than the population of Nazareth (probably around 1,000 strong), it was still a small town. Some estimate that from such a population it would have been a maximum of around 20 children who were likely to have been killed. Against the backdrop of Herod's other much more political atrocities, this event may not have stood out.

This in no way diminishes the appalling actions of Herod but may just explain why such an event was not recorded elsewhere (though for some its lack of external witness questions whether it did in fact happen). Matthew captures the terrible grief evoked by Herod's actions with the simple quote from Jeremiah 31.15: 'Thus says the Lord: A voice is heard in Ramah, lamentation and bitter weeping. Rachel is weeping for her children; she refuses to be comforted for her children, because they are no more.'

One of the important points to note, however, is that Jeremiah 31.15 is embedded in an otherwise entirely positive chapter that looks forward to the future time when God would redeem his people. At that time God will be the God of Israel once more and they will be his people (31.1); vineyards will be replanted (31.5) and people will worship at the temple again (31.6); the people will return with consolation (31.9) and there will be much dancing (31.13). This must surely have been in Matthew's mind as he wrote, since that time had indeed arrived. God had intervened to save his people but before the fruits of that redemption could be felt, a time of bitter weeping was upon them.

Matthew does not offer an indication of how long Joseph and Mary stayed in Egypt (an indication that would have helped in coming to a decision about the date of Jesus' birth), but it would not be unreasonable for this period to fit in with a 7/6 BC date of birth. The detail that Matthew offers about Joseph's reluctance to return to Judea because of Archelaus's rule there fits what is known from elsewhere. As we saw above (p. 100), Archelaus was eventually deposed because of his tyranny and brutality. That Joseph would fear this is entirely likely.

* * *

Reflection

One of the things about freedom is that, as human beings, we are really very bad at it. No sooner are we free than we find excuses to be slaves again. The Israelites did this in the wilderness. Barely had they crossed the Red Sea and seen the Egyptians die in their attempt to recapture them, than they began to reminisce about how they would have preferred to die in Egypt because at least they had food then (Exodus 16.3). Paul too explodes with frustration at the Galatians who, though freed by Christ, appear to want to resubmit themselves to a new slavery (Galatians 5.1).

With this in mind Matthew's message becomes even more powerful. Jesus went back to Egypt, to the place where God's people were first freed from slavery, so that the whole process could begin again. Like Moses, Jesus came to set us free. Unlike Moses he came to set us free from everything that enslaves us – not just the Egyptians. This new leader was someone who could give us freedom. Going back to Egypt, symbolically, reminds us of that freedom and of everything from which we need to be freed. For God's people that was slavery to the Egyptians; for us it is slavery of another kind – and sometimes it is a slavery that we have ourselves imposed. This Jesus came to lead us in a never to be repeated Exodus from all slavery of all kinds. The question we face is whether we can follow him to freedom and keep on following him, so that we do not re-enslave ourselves by what we think or do.

8

Simeon and Anna

The final moment in the birth narratives is the presentation of Jesus in the temple and his welcome by Simeon and Anna. Within the church calendar this event marks the end of the 40 days of the Christmas season and it seems an excellent place to end our reflections on the birth of Jesus.

Naming and Circumcision

> **Luke 2.21** After eight days had passed, it was time to circumcise the child; and he was called Jesus, the name given by the angel before he was conceived in the womb.

Verse 21 is often regarded by scholars as fitting better at the end of the birth narrative than here at the start of the presentation in the temple. The reality is that it doesn't really fit in either place and is a building block that moves us from Jesus' birth to his arrival in the temple for the first – though very much not the last – time. As in verse 1.59, Luke brought the naming and circumcision of Jesus together into a single event, even though there is no record of this happening together in Jewish custom. It is probably not worth pressing these details too hard. Luke wants to communicate that Jesus has been circumcised according to Jewish custom and named according to God's decree. Beyond this, further detail is unnecessary.

Purification

> **Luke 2.22-24** When the time came for their purification according to the law of Moses, they brought him up to Jerusalem to present him to the Lord [23](as it is written in the law of the Lord, 'Every firstborn male shall be designated as holy to the Lord'), [24]and they offered a sacrifice according to what is stated in the law of the Lord, 'a pair of turtle-doves or two young pigeons.'

Jewish law dictated that after a male birth a woman would be impure for seven days (in the case of a female birth the woman would be unclean for 14 days), and then should remain at home for a further 33 days, a period that was ended by a sacrifice offered in the temple at the Court of Women (according to the command in Leviticus 12.4 and 6). A number of commentators discuss the plural pronoun used here ('the time . . . for *their* purification'). It is clear from Jewish law that the one needing purification was the woman not the child, but since, even today, you would not leave a month-old child behind when travelling anywhere, it is not hard to see why Luke opted for that pronoun here.

The more interesting feature of verse 22 is Luke's observation that they had brought Jesus to the temple to present him to the Lord. The firstborn son was indeed required to be presented to God (see Exodus 13.2, 12 and 15; Numbers 3.13). The father of each firstborn was required to present a male firstborn child to God and then to buy him back with five shekels, as a symbol of the fact that he belonged to God. But this did not need to happen in the temple; it could have happened anywhere there was a priest.

It is not impossible that people did as Luke suggests Joseph did here, and combined the purification of the child's mother after childbirth with the symbolic offering and redemption of the firstborn in the temple itself. Locating the event in the temple also calls to mind the story of Samuel.

The action is also highly suggestive and sets up our expectations of the declaration of redemption that will be made in a few verses by Anna; just as Jesus has been redeemed here, so he too will redeem the whole world – though the cost of that will be very much greater than five shekels.

A pair of turtle-doves or two young pigeons

The purification of a mother required the offering of a lamb as a burnt offering and a pigeon or dove as a sin offering. Leviticus 12.8 allows for the offering to be two pigeons/doves in the case of poverty. Luke's passing comment here reminds us in the simplest possible way that Jesus was born into a poor not a wealthy household.

---

* * *

Reflection

With stories as rich as Luke's it is very easy to get carried away and read too much into them. My apologies in advance if you feel I have done this here, but there seems to me to be much on which we should reflect in the idea that Jesus was at the temple to be 'redeemed' by Joseph. Jesus the very Son of God was bought back by the man who was his adoptive father but not his biological father. Jesus was redeemed so that he could live like us. He was redeemed so that he could return to a life of rural poverty. He was redeemed so that his life would not be marked by the privilege of a temple, priestly upbringing.

Jesus was redeemed by an adoptive father who loved him, so that we could be redeemed by our own heavenly Father who loves us even more.

Simeon

> **Luke 2.25-35** Now there was a man in Jerusalem whose name was Simeon; this man was righteous and devout, looking forward to the consolation of Israel, and the Holy Spirit rested on him. [26]It had been revealed to him by the Holy Spirit that he would not see death before he had seen the Lord's Messiah. [27]Guided by the Spirit, Simeon came into the temple; and when the parents brought in the child Jesus, to do for him what was customary under the law, [28]Simeon took him in his arms and praised God, saying,
>
> [29]'Master, now you are dismissing your servant in peace,
> according to your word;
> [30]for my eyes have seen your salvation,
> [31]which you have prepared in the presence of all peoples,
> [32]a light for revelation to the Gentiles
> and for glory to your people Israel.'
>
> [33]And the child's father and mother were amazed at what was being said about him. [34]Then Simeon blessed them and said to his mother Mary, 'This child is destined for the falling and the rising of many in Israel, and to be a sign that will be opposed [35]so that the inner thoughts of many will be revealed – and a sword will pierce your own soul too.'

Guided by the Holy Spirit

Unfortunately we know very little at all about Simeon. All that Luke tells us, apart from his godliness, is that he lived in Jerusalem, that the Holy Spirit rested on him and that it then drove him into the temple at the right time to meet Jesus. We have already seen how important the action of the Holy Spirit was in

Luke's account even before the sending of the Spirit at Pentecost; here again the Spirit ensured that Simeon was in the right place at the right time to honour and greet Jesus.

From now on angels disappear from Luke's pages (until they return once more at the resurrection), but other characters come to fill their place. Simeon and Anna seem to be two iconic examples of human messengers. They recognized the significance of the event, they saw Jesus for who he really was and proclaimed their message far and wide. Luke seems to be suggesting to us that we too could be angels, declaring God's love in a world yearning for redemption and consolation.

One of the details that people assume of Simeon is that he was old. Indeed most of the works of art depicting him portray him as a very old man indeed. The reality is that Luke does not tell us this. Anna, as we shall see below, is very old, but Simeon's age is not declared at all. People tend to take the features associated with Anna and apply them to Simeon – she was very old, she was in the temple day and night, she had prepared herself with fasting and prayer. In contrast we know almost nothing about Simeon other than that he was righteous and devout and guided by the Spirit.

The only factors suggesting that Simeon was of an advanced age are that the Holy Spirit had revealed to him that he would not see death before he saw the Lord's Messiah and that he then asks God to let him depart in peace. It is probable but not certain that he was very old. The traditional interpretation may well be the correct one but it is worth asking ourselves the question of whether anything would change if Simeon were not, in fact, a very old man.

A lovely detail in the story is that Simeon did not just notice Jesus but took him in his arms. The Greek verb used here is *dechomai*, which means to receive. The word for arms here is a specific one, *agkalē*, used to describe an arm when it is bent to receive something. The point Luke seems to be making here is that Simeon was not only able to recognize salvation in the shape of a tiny baby but was ready in body, mind and spirit to receive that salvation himself. He bent his arm and held it out in preparation to receive the one in whom he saw salvation.

Righteous and devout

Strictly speaking we do not need both words here – 'righteous' and 'devout' are close to each other in meaning. What is important about them is that the word *dikaios* – translated 'righteous' – was drawn thoroughly from the Jewish tradition and was used of people who observed the law and all its commands. *Eulabēs* – translated 'devout' – had much more resonance in a Greek setting and referred to people who were reverent towards God, particularly as regards worship.

In other words whether you were Jewish or Greek, Simeon was to be regarded as a godly man. The characteristic that Luke tells us identifies him as righteous and devout is the fact that he looked forward to the consolation or comforting of Israel. The phrase is drawn from Isaiah 40.1, which declares comfort on God's people in exile – a comfort that involves them in welcoming God back into their midst. Nearly 500 years later Simeon still believed God's promise and actively looked out for its fulfilment. If righteousness has within it the virtue of faithfulness, then Simeon truly was a righteous man.

Nunc Dimittis

Simeon's beautiful song of praise, as with the Magnificat and the Benedictus, is commonly known by its Latin name, taken from the first words of the hymn. In terms of poetry, the Nunc Dimittis has a more clearly poetic form than the other Lukan hymns. Simeon's song is made up of three simple couplets: the first about Simeon's departure in peace; the second about the salvation he has seen; the third about the light that Jesus brought.

Master and slave

The popular translation of Simeon's song rather waters down the tone of what he said. The word normally translated 'Lord' is *despotēs* –

from which we get our English 'despot' – and refers to one who has control over others, especially slaves. The word translated 'servant' is *doulos*, or 'slave'. As a result Simeon is talking about a relationship in which he has felt compelled by a powerful master. There is no need to read into this unhappiness. Many slaves were content if their master was kind, but there is a strong sense here of compulsion and control. Simeon has felt compelled in his looking out for consolation and now feels released from that powerful grip.

The reason Simeon feels able to depart in peace is that his eyes have seen salvation. As we have observed elsewhere in the birth narratives, this recognition of salvation is important. Again, as a 40-day-old baby Jesus has not 'done' anything yet, but still Simeon can see salvation. Jesus' birth means that the world has been changed; God's intervention in the world has finally arrived; Simeon can depart peacefully because of the presence of Jesus. Jesus has not done anything – his presence in the midst of his people was enough.

Simeon's song picks up some of the themes of the angels' song to the shepherds. As we observed above, the angel's declaration of God's glory and of peace on earth was a declaration of God's glorious intervention in the world as the prophets foretold it. The time they have been waiting for has come. God has returned to his people as he promised he would.

Here this theme returns again. This time Simeon declares that God's salvation has been prepared before all peoples and that it will be a light for revelation to the Gentiles. One of Isaiah's key themes is that when God did intervene in the world the Gentiles would see it and recognize that he was God. A few of the verses below give a flavour of the type of expectation:

Psalm 98.2–3 The Lord has made known his victory; he has revealed his vindication in the sight of the nations. ³He has remembered his steadfast love and faithfulness to the house of Israel. All the ends of the earth have seen the victory of our God. **Isaiah 40.5** Then the glory of the Lord shall be revealed, and all people shall see it together, for the mouth of the Lord has spoken. **Isaiah 52.10** The Lord has bared his holy arm before the eyes of all the nations; and all the ends of the earth shall see the salvation of our God.

Not only would the nations see God's victory but this would bring glory to God's own people. The whole world would then recognize that God's people had been right all along, they would be vindicated in the eyes of the nations of the world. Simeon's song declares that with the birth of Jesus the long-awaited time has come.

The conversion of the Gentiles?

One of the points of debate between Jewish and Christian commentators on Isaiah's prophecies is what the Old Testament writers envisaged would happen to the nations once they had seen God's victory. For Christians the message of the inclusion of all who are drawn to God is so deeply ingrained that the assumption is that they would then be included in God's people and drawn into worshipping him.

The majority of Jews hold a different view. For them God is the God of his people – the Jews. As a result, when the Gentiles see God's victory it is simply that – seeing God's victory. Afterwards they would go on their way, convinced that God was God but not worshipping him and not converting to Judaism in order to do so.

The exchange is a fascinating one as it reveals a deep disagreement about the nature of conversion at the heart of our two faiths.

A sword will pierce your soul

At this point in Luke's story it is, to put it mildly, surprising to discover that Mary and Joseph marvelled at what Simeon said. Surely they were already primed about the extraordinary nature of the child Mary had borne. Some scholars take this as an indication that the birth narratives are a later fabrication, so that this was the first time they had heard anything about who Jesus was. It won't surprise you to know that I see another explanation for this.

The clue, it seems to me, is in the word *thaumazō*, which we explored a little above (see p. 112). While it can mean to be astonished or to marvel, it can also mean to wonder at something. It is indeed interesting that the word has been used three times already in Luke (1.21; 1.63; 2.18): when the crowd were waiting for Zechariah to emerge from the temple; when Zechariah wrote down John's name; when the shepherds had announced all that had happened. It may be that 'amazement' is the correct translation here but it is also possible that 'wonder' is a better rendering. If it is, then Mary and Joseph are simply carrying on 'pondering' as Luke told us Mary did in 2.19. The long string of marvellous things were simply too much to take in all at once – they needed pausing over, reflecting upon, and this is what Mary and Joseph did here.

* * *

Reflection

One of the greatest challenges facing us as we read the Christmas stories again and again is remembering simply how unexpected the birth of Jesus was. Of course the Jews were expecting a Messiah, and of course these expectations were combined with an expectation that the Messiah would be from the Davidic line and would be a king like David. They also expected that when this Messiah came he would drive out the Romans and re-establish the sovereignty, prosperity and peace of God's people. But that is all. Although there was some association at Qumran between the long-awaited Messiah and an angel, no one expected Jesus to be divine. No one expected him to be born in squalor and poverty. No one expected him to transform the world in the way he did.

It is easy, sometimes, to wonder why it took them all so long to catch on. Why did Mary and Joseph need to wonder again at what Simeon said – surely they were already prepared for such news? The answer is of course: they weren't. The mind-blowing unexpectedness of God's action was beyond any human comprehension. Indeed it is worth our trying to think back into what it might have felt like to be Mary or Joseph – or indeed anyone else who lived at the time of Jesus' birth. If we succeed then we just might recapture some of the wonder that God's unexpectedness really should evoke in us.

* * *

Simeon's blessing of Mary and Joseph mirrors what he said to God, though this is obscured in most translations. Taking the child in his arms he blessed God (the word used is *eulogeō*) and then turning to Mary and Joseph he blessed them (again the word *eulogeō* is used). This may help to explain the rather odd – and profoundly depressing – blessing that Simeon utters. Blessing does not include saying nice things about someone, it involves deep insight and the recognition of the truth that lies before you. Proclaiming blessing involves declaring the truth that might otherwise remain unsaid. In this case the truth is that the world has changed and the longed-for time has come. It is also the truth that Jesus' very being will bring judgement. In a similar way to Mary's Magnificat, Simeon's Nunc Dimittis declares that there will be those who will be raised up and those who will be cast down – that is the truth of who Jesus really was.

It is a truth that recognizes that such a person will bring with him turmoil and heartache. Mary his mother must steel herself for all that is to come. Jesus the light has come to shine in the darkness but those whose lives are lived under cover of darkness will not welcome the light that he brings. Again we are reminded of Herod in Matthew's account; this is a similar message. Matthew revealed the responses Jesus could expect by casting a vignette of a single, powerful person's response; Luke hints at the same thing but in more general terms.

Anna

The final but by no means least of the characters we meet in the birth narratives is Anna. We noted above how easy it is to transfer the characteristics of Anna on to Simeon. Anna is the one declared to be very old. Anna is the prophet. Anna fasted and prayed in the temple. Although Simeon is in many people's minds the more dominant character in that part of the story (not least because of the Nunc Dimittis), we know much more about Anna than we do about Simeon.

> **Luke 2.36–39** There was also a prophet, Anna the daughter of Phanuel, of the tribe of Asher. She was of a great age, having lived with her husband for seven years after her marriage, 37then as a widow to the age of eighty-four. She never left the temple but worshipped there with fasting and prayer night and day.
> 38At that moment she came, and began to praise God and to speak about the child to all who were looking for the redemption of Jerusalem. 39When they had finished everything required by the law of the Lord, they returned to Galilee, to their own town of Nazareth.

The name Anna is the Greek version of the Hebrew name Hannah. We are told that she was from the tribe of Asher, which was one of the ten northern tribes, and that she was a prophet. These details are important. That she was from the north emphasizes the fact that she was not in the temple by accident. She did not, like Simeon, live locally and was guided to the temple by the Holy Spirit. Instead she was dedicated and lived there permanently as part of her vocation as prophet. Sadly Luke does not tell us either what she said about Jesus or what she said about other topics, but the implication is that she was a powerful, dedicated and faithful woman.

The grammar of verse 36 is not easy to interpret. Some argue that it means that she was 84. The more likely reading of the Greek is that she had been married for seven years and a widow for 84 years. If she married at 12 then this means that she was about 103. In a sense it doesn't really matter: she was either really quite old or very old, and had prepared herself for Jesus' arrival in the temple.

Unlike Simeon she did not greet Jesus personally but instead began to proclaim who he was to everyone who was looking for the 'redemption of Israel'. This phrase can be seen to be similar to the phrase used of Simeon – someone who was looking for the consolation of Israel; in other words anyone who was alert to the action of God in the world.

* * *

Reflection

The contrast between Simeon and Anna is an interesting one. One person, Simeon, arrived on the scene because of the actions of the Holy Spirit. The other, Anna, was there already, ready and waiting, prepared by disciplined prayer and fasting. One greeted the child personally; the other simply proclaimed who he was to anyone who would listen. But both recognized the same thing: that before them in the form of a tiny baby lay Israel's redemption.

A question that lies implicitly beneath the whole of the Gospel narrative is the question of why some people recognized who Jesus was when others did not. Luke suggests to us here two models of people who were able to see Jesus for who he really was: one was someone on whom the Spirit descended; the other a faithful servant of God whose lengthy preparation prepared her to recognize God in the most unexpected of forms. Those who could not recognize him for who he was were those who were deaf to the proclamation of angelic-type figures – whether earthly or heavenly – and those who had too much to lose.

The question that haunts me from this passage is whether I would be able to recognize God in the most unexpected of guises or whether, caught up by busyness, anxiety and power, I might go on my way without even noticing the presence of God in our midst.

Matthew and Luke – and John – have brought us on a long journey from the very dawn of time, through the peaks and troughs of the story of God's people to the time of Jesus' birth. We have travelled with them through decades and centuries of hope and expectation until we saw the fulfilment of those years of preparation in its most unexpected form – a king born in poverty; a leader in the form of a baby; a saviour who has done nothing as yet but be present, God in fragile human form. At the end of this journey we recognize the truth of God, that no matter how long we wait, how fervently we hope, how diligently we expect – God will always surprise and appear in a manner we least expect. Our task, like that of Anna, is to become sentinels of God's kingdom so attuned to the things of God that no matter how unexpected his appearance we are able to see, perceive and proclaim God's redemption of the world he created.

Meditation

In unexpected form, God came
  to an unexpected Mother,
  in unexpected poverty

But still some recognized him
  Some came drawn by angel song
  others by a star
  One came guided by the Spirit

But one sat waiting for him,
  day after day
  night after night
  fasting and praying
  for 84 long years she waited
  waiting to greet her God

God still comes in unexpected form,
  at unexpected times in unexpected ways
  May we, with the spirit of Anna, be ready and waiting when
    he does.

Questions for Bible Study/Advent Groups

I often hesitate to offer questions for Bible Study groups since each group is unique and will want to explore the material in their own way. Nevertheless some people may like to use the material in this book to stimulate discussion and reflection during Advent, and some of you may value the springboard into discussion that questions can offer. The questions below are conversation starters based around each chapter of the book. I expect that once you get going you will find your own way through the material, so do use as many or as few of these as are helpful. Depending on how talkative your group is, you may need more questions than are given below. I hope you will see them as suggestive rather than prescriptive, and that you will raise whichever questions have emerged for you and your group in your reflections on the passages.

Some groups will want to study all of the passages in each chapter but others will find that too much, so under each chapter I suggest which passage you might like to focus on if you wish to read a passage in your group, with questions on that particular passage as well as further questions on the chapter as a whole.

There are of course lots of other questions you could ask but these should get the conversation going. I would also recommend that each time you take some time to discuss what the particular passage tells you about the incarnation, God with us. What can we learn about the nature of God and about who Jesus came to be from these passages?

Part 1: Origins

Focus on: John 1.1–18

Questions around this passage:

- What kind of literature do you think John 1.1–18 is? A poem? A hymn? A theological reflection? Do you have a view on whether it was written by the same author who wrote the rest of the Gospel?
- What is it, do you think, about Genesis 1 that has so captured the minds of the authors of the New Testament, but here especially John?
- What does it mean for you for Jesus to be described as The Word of God, the *logos*?

Broader questions:

- Why do you think Matthew included the four women in his genealogy?
- Why are genealogies/family trees so important to people?
- Does it bother you that Matthew and Luke's genealogies are not the same?

Part 2: Announcements

Focus on: Luke 1.26–38

- Does the knowledge that Mary may have been as young as 11–12 change your view of her in any way?
- What issues are raised for you by the discussion of the virginal conception/virgin birth of Jesus? How important is it as a doctrine for our understanding of Jesus?
- Why do you think Mary was so greatly troubled by Gabriel's greeting: 'Greetings/Rejoice favoured one'?

You might like to go on to talk about the Magnificat from here.

- Is it a song that resonates with you? Why? Which are your favourite bits?
- Why do you think there is so much Old Testament in Mary's song?

Broader questions:

- Do you think it was fair for Zechariah to lose the ability to speak due to his response to the angel?
- What effect does the wrapping of the announcement of Jesus' birth in the announcement and birth of John the Baptist have on this important passage?
- Compare the Benedictus (Zechariah's song) with the Magnificat (Mary's song). What is similar and what is different about them? Which do you prefer?
- Why do you think announcement/prophecy is so important, especially to Luke at this stage of his Gospel?

Part 3: Arrivals

Focus on: Luke 2.8–20

- What do you think is the importance of the shepherds being the first to hear of Jesus' birth?
- Talk about glory and peace (the message of the angels). Why was this announcement so important?
- Spend some time on the three titles – Saviour, Messiah, Lord. What does each of them say about who Jesus was?

Broader questions:

- Why do you think Luke doesn't tell us that John's name meant 'God has shown favour'?

- Imagine what Elizabeth might have to say about everything that happened. If she were telling you about it, what kind of things might she say? Then you might like to imagine what Mary had to say too!
- Does it make very much difference to you if Jesus was *not* born in a stable but in a family home and placed in a feeding trough on the lower floor?

Part 4: Aftermaths

Focus on: Matthew 2.1–8

- What insights into the passage does knowing some of Herod's backstory give you?
- What do you think is most important about the magi? That they were Gentiles? That they were astrologers/wise men? That they were regarded as magicians? That they had travelled a long way? That they revealed Jesus' birth to Herod? Something else?
- Reflect on the contrast between Matthew and Luke's accounts concerning the shepherds/magi visiting Jesus after his birth. Why do you think Luke chose to tell us about the shepherds and Matthew about the magi?

Broader questions:

- Do you think it is important that angels disappear from Luke's account after Jesus' birth until the resurrection?
- What do you think Simeon was saying in his song (Nunc Dimittis)?
- Why are Simeon and Anna so important in this story?

For Further Reading

There are surprisingly few books on the birth narratives themselves.

For commentaries, you need to look at the relevant Gospel commentary.

Some of the best books on the birth narratives include the following.

Borg, Marcus J., *The First Christmas: What the Gospels Really Teach Us About Jesus's Birth*, London: SPCK, 2008.

Brooke, George J. (ed.), *The Birth of Jesus: Biblical and Theological Reflections*, Edinburgh: T. & T. Clark, 2000.

Brown, R., *The Birth of the Messiah: A Commentary on the Infancy Narratives in the Gospels of Matthew and Luke*, updated edition, New York: Yale University Press, 2007 (there is also a much shorter version of this which is a digest of what Brown said – see Brown, Raymond E., *An Adult Christ at Christmas*, Collegeville, MN: Liturgical Press, 1978.)

Freed, Edwin D., *Stories of Jesus' Birth: A Critical Introduction*, Sheffield: Sheffield Academic Press, 2001.

Horsley, Richard A., *Liberation of Christmas: Infancy Narratives in Social Context*, New York: Crossroad Publishing, 1987.

Moyise, Steve, *Was the Birth of Jesus According to Scripture?*, Eugene, OR: Cascade Books, 2013.

Biblical Index

Page numbers in bold indicate an extended treatment of the passage.

Old Testament